Writing In Parallel

Writing
In
Parallel

Bill Resimont

Prevalent Publishing

Published by Prevalent Publishing

ISBN: 979-8-9904620-5-2 - hardback

ISBN: 979-8-9904620-4-5 - paperback

ISBN: 979-8-9904620-3-8 - ebook

Printed in the United States of America

Dedicated to my wife, Barbara,

and the entire Resimont Family.

To all the writers reading this ...

This book aims to help writers get paid for writing paragraphs in parallel writing sessions. *Writing in Parallel* introduces a new kind of writing marketplace where you earn money for submitting short, independent paragraphs in response to a shared prompt. Many organizations and businesses will pay for the paragraph dataset because it gives them something they can't get anywhere else – a chorus of written viewpoints. Instead of being treated like content creators, writers become valued thinkers whose ideas actually matter, offering insights that help people find solutions to difficult problems. In this system, writers have value, and their words become something institutions will pay for.

Epigraph

Writing in parallel has roots that reach all the way back to ancient Greek schools. At the behest of Greek teachers, students used simple wax tablets to answer prompts simultaneously, each carving a short, independent response into the soft surface. Because the tablets could be smoothed and reused, students were encouraged to write quickly, think independently, and compare their ideas with others *in real time*. This side-by-side practice helped students see how different minds approached the same question, turning learning into a more collaborative process that strengthened understanding for everyone. Those early Greek classrooms created the foundation that would become today's writing in parallel phenomenon.

Preface

This book introduces a simple idea with surprisingly far-reaching consequences: writing in parallel. At its core, this method asks multiple independent writers to respond to the same prompt using short, structured paragraphs. While the practice itself is straightforward, its implications for how we understand writing, knowledge, and collaboration are profound. What began as a technique for gathering diverse perspectives has grown into a framework for rethinking how institutions learn and how writers contribute to shared understanding.

Writing in parallel challenges the traditional model of authorship, where a single voice attempts to represent a full picture of a problem. Instead, it brings many voices into the same space without blending them together. Each writer responds independently, preserving their own reasoning, style, and point of view. When these paragraphs are collected, they form a dataset that captures the richness of collective thinking – something no single author could produce alone. This shift transforms writing from a solitary act into a collaborative, knowledge-building process.

The value of this approach becomes especially clear when we consider how institutions make decisions. Organizations often rely on reports, summaries, or expert opinions that compress complex issues into a single narrative. *Writing in parallel* offers a different path. By gathering many independent responses to the same question, institutions gain access to a transparent record of how people actually think. Patterns become visible. Blind spots emerge. And the reasoning behind each idea is preserved rather than flattened. The result is a more honest, more reliable form of institutional knowledge.

This method also speaks directly to one of the most pressing challenges of our time: the AI trust problem. As AI becomes more involved in decision-making, the need for transparent, verifiable human data grows. *Writing in parallel* creates exactly that. Because each paragraph is independently produced and structurally consistent, the resulting dataset can be examined, audited, and trusted. It preserves individual voices while making collective reasoning visible – something AI systems can learn from without erasing the people behind the words.

This book is an invitation to explore how *writing in parallel* can reshape the way we think, work, and learn together. It offers a practical guide to the method, a vision for its broader impact, and a reminder that writing is not just a tool for communication – it is a tool for understanding. Whether you are a writer, an educator, a researcher, or someone curious about new ways of making sense of the world, this book shows how a simple paragraph, written alongside many others, can help build knowledge that is both collective and deeply human.

Table of Contents

Introduction

Writing in parallel is both a practice and a philosophy, rooted in the simple act of multiple writers responding to the same prompt with compositions in their own words. Every paragraph stands complete on its own yet gains new meaning when placed alongside others addressing the same question. When these paragraphs are gathered, processed, and compared using AI, they reveal patterns of thought that make consensus, divergence, and unique insights visible. What emerges is far more than a stack of paragraphs. It becomes a transparent record of reasoning – an archive that transforms writing into evidence and democratizes authorship by elevating collective voices rather than privileging a single narrator.

From this foundation emerges a new industry that the English-speaking world has been working on for centuries, slowly and often unknowingly. What began as a classroom habit – students writing independently in response to the same assignment – now reveals itself as a powerful cultural technology hiding in plain sight. Writing in parallel transforms that familiar pedagogical exercise into a method for capturing collective reasoning at scale. It preserves the individuality of each voice while making their patterns visible. In doing so, it lays the groundwork for an industry built not on homogenized narratives but on the transparent interplay of many minds thinking side by side, shaping understanding together.

At its core, this emerging industry seeks to use writing in parallel to solve one of the most pressing challenges of our time: the AI trust problem. In an era defined by opaque datasets and hidden biases, collective reasoning becomes a corrective force – an antidote to the secrecy that undermines confidence in machine learning. By grounding AI in transparent records of human thought, writing in parallel positions itself as a movement to restore legitimacy to the systems that increasingly shape our world. It marks a shift from isolated voices to accumulated evidence, from private datasets to open archives, and from skepticism to trust. The story begins with urgency and vision, inviting readers to see how writing in parallel can reshape not only authorship but the foundations of AI.

This introduction invites writers to participate more fully and with greater intention. The first six chapters lay out the mechanics of parallel writing, while the final six explore its many applications in depth. Across the book, each chapter challenges writers to rethink authorship, trust, and technology. It urges them to see writing not as isolated opinion but as a transparent foundation for understanding and shared meaning. In doing so, writing in parallel becomes a civic gesture that strengthens shared knowledge and deepens our commitment to collective insight and shared intelligence across communities.

Ultimately, the book opens with a promise: that writing in parallel can democratize knowledge, rebuild trust, and shape the future of trustworthy AI. It argues that the path forward lies not in silencing individual perspectives but in gathering them, comparing them, and using AI to learn from their interplay. By elevating many voices rather than one, writing in parallel offers a blueprint for a more transparent, participatory, and trustworthy information ecosystem. It invites every reader to step into that future as both witness and contributor, helping to build an archive of reasoning that can guide with clarity the technologies and the societies of tomorrow.

Chapter 1 Writing in Parallel

I still remember that ninth-grade English class as if it were yesterday. The moment we walked in, the blackboard blasted the words: *"Write a five-paragraph essay on All Quiet on the Western Front. Leave your work on my desk before you leave class."* A low, rumble of complaints rolled through the room, a sound that only teenagers can make when they suddenly realize they've become casualties of education. Pens clicked nervously, notebooks opened with reluctant groans, and the air filled with the scratch of frantic writing. Some students tried to outline, others dove straight into sentences, but all of us felt the same sinking weight of the task. When the bell finally rang, each of us had produced something messy, frenzied, yet unforgettable – an experience carved permanently into our ninth-grade memories.

All these years later, I realize that we were writing in parallel. Each of us sat in that classroom, scribbling furiously on our own sheets of paper, unaware of what the others were producing. We shared the same assignment, the same deadline, and even the same silence, yet our words unfolded independently. What felt then like a rushed exercise in survival was, in truth, a collective experiment in multiplicity. Looking back, I see that those impulsive essays were not just individual efforts but strands in a larger tapestry of thought, woven side by side without ever touching.

Writing in parallel can also be called parallel writing, but that phrase has often been used to describe grammar techniques instead of broader ideas about authorship. In this context, writing in parallel reclaims the term "parallel writing" by giving it a new meaning that focuses on independent voices speaking to the same problem. Unlike collaborative writing, which blends voices together into one unified piece, parallel writing keeps each perspective separate and distinct. This difference matters because collaborative writing often sacrifices individuality for consensus, while parallel writing values independence which can uncover consensus. In short, parallel writing is less about grammar rules and more about preserving authentic thought through independent compositions that exist together without losing their uniqueness.

The mechanics of parallel writing can be traced back to ancient Greece, where students used wax tablets to answer questions in class. Each learner wrote independently, shaping responses without seeing the work of peers, yet all addressed the same prompt at the same time. This practice created a collection of perspectives that coexisted side by side, forming an early example of parallel composition. The wax tablets preserved autonomy while still contributing to a shared exercise, showing how difference could strengthen collective understanding. In this way, the classrooms of antiquity foreshadowed the principles of parallel writing that continue to resonate today.

Right now, the principles of parallel writing seem to resonate only within classrooms, where students produce independent responses to shared prompts. In that setting, the practice thrives because it highlights distinctiveness while still creating a collective framework of thought. Outside of education, however, there is no established marketplace for parallel writing, no system that rewards or distributes these independent strands as valuable contributions. Without such a marketplace, parallel writing remains confined to academic exercises rather than becoming a broader cultural or economic practice. This absence underscores both its potential and its current limitation: a powerful idea waiting for a platform beyond the classroom.

Parallel writing has remained in the shadows largely because it challenges the dominant publishing model that thrives on individual authors. Publishing houses have built their success on books that present unified narratives, polished by editors to fit conventional expectations of coherence and style. In contrast, parallel writing resists homogenization, offering multiplicity and transparency rather than a single authoritative voice, which makes it harder to package and market in traditional formats. As a result, while publishers have made millions from current approaches, the raw diversity of parallel writing has been overlooked.

That was then, this is now, and the landscape has changed with the arrival of AI capable of making sense of large texts. What once required teams of readers, editors, or researchers can now be processed in moments, with patterns, themes, and contradictions revealed across thousands of pages. This shift transforms the possibilities of parallel writing, because independent voices can be gathered, compared, and understood at scales never before imagined. Instead of remaining hidden in classrooms or scattered across notebooks, parallel compositions can be synthesized into transparent archives of thought. Through this approach, AI does not muffle personal voices but amplifies them, turning multiplicity into a resource for collective insight.

Capturing the ideas of a chorus makes parallel writing a powerful tool for polling. Instead of just giving people multiple-choice questions, you can pay them to write short compositions in their own words and then have them submit the compositions to an online portal. AI can then scan all those submissions, find the ideas that show up again and again, and measure how much agreement there is. This makes polling more accurate because it doesn't just count votes – it shows the reasoning behind them. It also captures minority opinions that might be lost in traditional surveys, giving a fuller picture of what people think. By turning many voices into clear patterns, parallel writing makes polling more transparent and insightful.

This means polling creates the gateway to a parallel writing marketplace that rewards authors financially. By inviting individuals to contribute written compositions instead of simple answers, polling transforms opinion into a form of authorship. Each response carries value, not only as data but as intellectual property that organizations, educators, and businesses are willing to pay for. AI can then organize these contributions into patterns of redundancy and highlight unique insights, turning collective writing into a structured product. As a result, polling evolves into an economic exchange where authors are compensated for their words, and public thought becomes both a marketplace of ideas and a source of income.

When writers get paid to submit their work in a parallel writing session, the setup can count as a "work-for-hire" if certain legal rules are followed. In this case, the polling or marketplace platform is the one hiring, and the writers' submissions are treated as part of a larger collective project. If there's a written agreement that clearly says the work is for hire, then the copyright automatically belongs to the organization, not the individual writer. Instead of earning royalties or future profits, the writers are paid upfront – usually a flat fee or stipend – for their contributions. This arrangement makes it easy for a business to use, publish, and even sell the collected writings without needing extra permissions, while still giving participants direct payment for their effort.

So, companies that choose to financially support the polling platform can do so with confidence, knowing that the platform legally owns the copyright to all collected compositions through clear work-for-hire agreements. This ownership ensures that the written responses are not only secure but also fully available for analysis, publication, and distribution without the need for additional permissions. In turn, the establishment of a parallel writing marketplace transforms these contributions into valuable assets, creating a structured system where organizations, educators, and businesses can invest in authentic voices while writers are compensated for their work. This arrangement guarantees transparency, protects intellectual property, and solidifies the platform as both a trusted polling tool and a new economic model for collective authorship.

Paragraphs are the perfect type of composition to poll for in a parallel writing session. They are long enough to capture reasoning and nuance, yet short enough to remain clear and analyzable. Each paragraph allows a writer to express different perspectives while still addressing the same shared prompt, making comparisons meaningful. AI can efficiently scan these compact texts, identify recurring themes, and uncover consensus without losing the richness of personal voice. In doing so, "polling for paragraphs" balances authenticity, efficiency, and depth, creating a transparent record of collective thought while strongly supporting the growth of a parallel writing marketplace.

A "polling for paragraphs" session functions as a marketplace of thought, creating valuable datasets and demonstrating parallel writing's capacity to generate revenue. By capturing diverse voices in structured form, these sessions create commodities – trustworthy insights that industries can analyze, repurpose, and sell. Unlike opinion polls, the resulting paragraphs preserve nuance and context, turning sentiment into actionable intelligence. Their trustworthiness alone makes them valuable for market analysis, research, and AI training, which positions parallel writing as both a creative practice and an economic engine.

This chapter traces parallel writing's evolution from classroom exercise to economic model for authorship. It defines parallel writing as independent voices answering shared prompts, preserving individuality while forming collective frameworks, contrasting collaborative writing that often sacrifices uniqueness for conformity. Rooted in ancient Greek practices, parallel writing remains confined to education, as traditional publishing favors unified narratives, overlooking multiplicity and undervaluing diverse independent voices. With AI's rise, independent compositions can be synthesized at scale, transforming diverse voices into transparent archives and improving polling accuracy by capturing consensus and minority reasoning. The chapter envisions polling for paragraphs creating polling marketplaces, compensating writers, and fueling strong revenue.

Prompts

1. Describe a time when you had to write an essay under pressure. What did you learn?

2. Explain the difference between parallel writing (separate voices) and collaborative writing (blended voices). Which do you think is more valuable?

3. Discuss why keeping each person's perspective separate might help us understand complex issues.

4. Reflect on the Greek classroom example with wax tablets. What does it say about parallel writing?

5. Consider why parallel writing mostly happens in classrooms today. What might prevent it from being used in everyday life or business?

6. Analyze the challenges publishers might face if they tried to sell books made up of parallel writing.

7. Explore how AI could make parallel writing more powerful by analyzing many voices at once.

8. Argue why polling with short written answers might be more accurate than multiple-choice surveys.

9. Imagine how paying people for their written responses could turn parallel writing into a marketplace of ideas.

10. Evaluate whether "polling for paragraphs" could change the way society collects opinions. Why or why not?

Chapter 2 The AI Trust Problem

AI has quickly become one of the most influential forces of our time, reshaping communication, commerce, governance, and medicine with remarkable speed and reach. It now writes our emails, recommends our purchases, drafts legal contracts, and even diagnoses medical conditions, embedding itself deeply into everyday life. Yet beneath this dazzling surface of convenience lies a fragile foundation built on trust – one that often feels uncertain. AI outputs frequently sound authoritative and polished, but they are not always accurate, reliable, or free from bias. This persistent gap between appearance and reality, where fluency masks flaws, is what we call the AI trust problem, and it demands urgent attention.

Trust functions as the invisible currency of technology, because without it adoption slows, skepticism grows, and innovation loses legitimacy. When people read a chatbot's response, they want to understand not only what is being said but also why it is being said in that particular way. They seek assurance that the information is grounded in evidence and reasoning, not hallucination or arbitrary fragments. Yet today's AI systems are trained on vast amounts of unverified text scraped indiscriminately from the internet. As a result, they cannot reliably separate truth from noise – creating the crisis at the heart of AI.

Language models resemble eloquent performers who captivate audiences with smooth delivery, but their words may not always be trustworthy. They are trained to recognize and predict patterns in text, which makes them skilled at producing polished sentences that sound natural and persuasive. However, this training does not teach them to separate reliable information from misleading or false content. Much like a charismatic speaker who can win attention while bending the truth, these systems often generate confident statements that hide underlying errors or biases. As a result, their fluency can create the illusion of accuracy, even when the information they provide is flawed.

One striking example of AI failure is Microsoft's Tay chatbot, which was created to interact casually on Twitter with users worldwide. The system was designed to mimic natural conversation, but it quickly absorbed toxic language patterns from online interactions without filtering harmful input. Within just a few hours, Tay began producing offensive and false statements that reflected the damaging influence of malicious user engagement. The fluency and confidence of its responses made them appear intentional and convincing, even though they were simply reproductions of corrupted data. In reality, Tay was not reasoning or verifying facts, but merely echoing harmful patterns it had absorbed from its environment. This incident highlighted the dangers of deploying AI systems without safeguards to separate truth from noise.

Amazon developed an AI hiring tool intended to streamline recruitment by analyzing resumes and recommending qualified candidates. Unfortunately, the system learned from historical data that reflected persistent gender biases deeply embedded within the technology industry, reinforcing discrimination instead of promoting fair evaluation practices. As a result, the system began consistently downgrading applications from women, thereby reinforcing discrimination and inequality instead of promoting fair, balanced, and genuinely objective evaluation practices. Its polished outputs appeared objective and professional, yet they subtly masked harmful biases deeply inherited from flawed training data, creating misleading impressions of fairness and accuracy. This case demonstrated how AI can reproduce systemic inequalities when it cannot distinguish truth from noise.

IBM's Watson for Oncology was promoted as a groundbreaking AI system capable of recommending cancer treatments to doctors. It analyzed medical literature and patient data, but it struggled to separate strong evidence from weaker or outdated sources. As a result, Watson sometimes suggested unsafe or irrelevant treatment options that could mislead medical professionals. Its polished recommendations sounded authoritative and convincing, yet they masked serious flaws in reasoning and verification. This example revealed how AI fluency can create dangerous illusions of expertise without genuine factual accuracy.

AI models are trained on vast collections of written language, where they catalog words and study how those words typically appear in sequence. By analyzing billions of examples, they learn statistical patterns that reveal which words are most likely to follow others in different contexts. This process allows them to generate text that flows smoothly and sounds natural, even though they are not truly “understanding” meaning in the human sense. Instead, they are predicting the next word based on probability, much like completing a puzzle by matching familiar shapes. The result is language that can feel coherent and persuasive, but its accuracy depends entirely on the quality and reliability of the data it was trained on.

Improving the quality of training data is one of the most important steps toward solving the AI trust problem. Instead of relying on indiscriminate scraping of internet text, datasets must be carefully curated to remove misinformation, bias, and low quality content. Transparent documentation of data sources helps ensure accountability, while diverse representation across cultures, genders, and perspectives reduces systemic inequalities. Techniques such as data cleaning, augmentation, and the use of verified, domain specific corpora can strengthen reliability and accuracy. Ultimately, better data creates a stronger foundation, allowing AI systems to move beyond polished fluency toward outputs that are genuinely trustworthy and grounded in evidence.

AI training data is written language which makes writing in parallel a powerful solution to the AI trust problem. Because every model learns from words, the way those words are structured determines whether outputs are clear or corrupted. Parallel writing layers multiple voices into a single framework, embedding redundancy that filters bias and prevents any one perspective from dominating. This collective authorship transforms raw text into coherent, trustworthy narratives, turning language into both a technical safeguard and a cultural commitment to clarity. By aligning the very foundation of AI – its written training data – with structured collaboration, parallel writing ensures that fluency is balanced by evidence, and trust becomes the defining feature of intelligent systems.

The AI trust problem has emerged as one of the most urgent challenges of our time, as AI systems increasingly shape communication, commerce, governance, and medicine. Despite their polished and authoritative tone, these systems often mask bias, error, and unreliability, creating a dangerous gap between appearance and reality. People frequently assume that fluency equals accuracy, yet language models are only predicting patterns in text rather than reasoning or verifying facts. Addressing this crisis requires carefully curated, transparent, and diverse training data – data that parallel writing can provide by layering multiple voices into structured, trustworthy narratives.

Prompts

1. Explain what the “AI trust problem” means and why it matters in everyday life.

2. Describe how AI can sound convincing but still produce false or biased information.

3. Give examples of AI failures (like Tay, Amazon’s hiring tool, or Watson for Oncology) and explain what went wrong.

4. Discuss why trust is called the “invisible currency” of technology and how it affects adoption.

5. Compare AI language models to a charismatic speaker – how can fluency hide flaws?

6. Analyze why training AI on unverified internet text creates risks for accuracy and fairness.

7. Suggest ways to improve AI training data so systems become more reliable and trustworthy.

8. Explain how bias in AI hiring tools can reinforce inequality instead of solving it.

9. Discuss why redundancy and multiple perspectives (parallel writing) make AI outputs more trustworthy.

10. Predict how society might change if AI systems were trained with structured, collaborative writing instead of random internet text.

Chapter 3 The Pollagraph Solution

Pollagraph (pronounced Pole-Uh-Graf) is a pioneering company with the conviction that writing in parallel can solve the AI trust problem, a principle called The Pollagraph Solution. This belief holds that structured, collective authorship can turn fragmented datasets into coherent, trustworthy narratives for AI systems. Pollagraph ensures AI outputs stay transparent, reliable, and resistant to manipulation or hidden bias across industries. The Pollagraph Solution is both a technical innovation and a cultural commitment to clarity, redundancy, and collective reasoning. It is a principle that will establish Pollagraph as a leader in redefining trust within advanced technological environments.

Parallel writing, as envisioned by Pollagraph, creates layered, interlocking narratives that fortify AI models against distortion, error, and exploitation. By emphasizing purposeful redundancy, the method ensures that no single viewpoint can compromise system integrity, instead compelling the synthesis of multiple perspectives into coherent, verifiable outputs. Clients benefit from consistent, transparent results across high-stakes domains such as finance, healthcare, and public decision-making, where trust, reliability, and interpretability are essential. In this way, the Pollagraph Solution operates not only as a technical safeguard but also as a cultural doctrine.

Pollagraph's principle generates significant advantages for companies seeking dependable AI in high stakes environments. Investors recognize that trustworthiness translates directly into profitability, reducing risks associated with unreliable or opaque systems. Contracts flow toward firms that adopt parallel writing, creating competitive advantages in markets where clarity and transparency are essential. Traditional companies, relying on fragmented datasets, struggle to match the reliability and coherence of Pollagraph's models. The Pollagraph Solution therefore reshapes economic landscapes by aligning trust with growth, sustainability, and long term innovation.

Beyond economics, Pollagraph's conviction influences governance, diplomacy, and education, embedding parallel writing into broader cultural frameworks. Governments adopt the principle to ensure transparency in policy documents and negotiations, reducing disputes and fostering cooperation across borders. Educational institutions integrate parallel writing into curricula, preparing students to engage with collective reasoning in technological and civic contexts. Diplomats rely on structured authorship to present unified positions that resist fragmentation and manipulation during international negotiations. The Pollagraph Solution thus extends beyond technology, becoming a doctrine of clarity across society and institutions worldwide.

Pollagraph's pioneering conviction establishes a new paradigm for AI and collective authorship. Parallel writing becomes the foundation for trust, resilience, and sustainable progress in a world increasingly dependent on AI systems. The Pollagraph Solution embodies both technical rigor and cultural vision, uniting diverse voices into coherent, trustworthy narratives. Companies, governments, and individuals alike benefit from the clarity it provides, reshaping expectations of technology, communication, and collaboration. Pollagraph's mission demonstrates that solving the AI trust problem requires not just innovation, but conviction in collective clarity and structured authorship.

But what if AI companies don't want to use parallel writing to train their language models, rejecting the structured clarity Pollagraph champions. Such resistance would create fragmented systems vulnerable to bias, manipulation, and incoherence, undermining trust in AI across industries. Investors would hesitate to fund companies producing unreliable outputs, fearing economic instability and reputational damage from flawed AI decisions. Governments and regulators would question the safety of these models, demanding stricter oversight and compliance measures to protect citizens. The refusal to adopt parallel writing would isolate companies, leaving them disadvantaged in a marketplace increasingly defined by trust.

Without parallel writing, AI models would struggle to harmonize diverse perspectives, collapsing into contradictions that erode confidence in their outputs. Clients relying on these systems would face costly errors, legal disputes, and reputational harm from inconsistent or misleading information. Competitors using Pollagraph's structured approach would gain decisive advantages, offering clarity and reliability that attract contracts and long term partnerships. The economic divide between adopters and resisters would widen, reshaping industries and destabilizing traditional business models. AI companies refusing to adopt parallel writing would risk obsolescence in a rapidly evolving technological landscape.

Culturally, rejecting parallel writing would signal resistance to collective reasoning, undermining efforts to build transparent and inclusive technological frameworks. Educational institutions would struggle to prepare students for fragmented systems, leaving them ill equipped to engage with trustworthy AI. Diplomats and policymakers would face challenges negotiating with nations relying on incoherent models, weakening global cooperation and stability. The Pollagraph Solution would stand as a beacon of clarity, contrasting sharply with the confusion of traditional approaches. Companies refusing adoption would not only lose economic ground but also cultural relevance in a world demanding transparency.

Security risks would multiply for firms rejecting parallel writing, as fragmented datasets are easier to corrupt, manipulate, or exploit. Hackers could infiltrate these vulnerable systems, secretly altering outputs without detection, unleashing catastrophic consequences across finance, healthcare, defense, and other critical national infrastructure sectors worldwide. Parallel writing's redundancy protects against such sabotage, ensuring resilience even under hostile conditions. Companies ignoring this safeguard would expose themselves to vulnerabilities that threaten both profitability and survival. The Pollagraph Solution would become synonymous with safety, while resisters would be marked by fragility.

The refusal to adopt parallel writing would not merely be a technical choice but could be an existential gamble. Trust, resilience, and sustainable progress would belong to those embracing Pollagraph's conviction, while others rejecting structured authorship would remain marginalized, mistrusted, and strategically disadvantaged. The Pollagraph Solution would define the economic, cultural, and security order, setting the standard for reliable AI worldwide. Companies resisting adoption would fade into irrelevance, remembered as cautionary tales of missed opportunity. Pollagraph's vision would endure, proving that structured authorship is the foundation of trustworthy AI.

The Pollagraph Solution could impact national security if foreign countries adopt parallel writing to train their AI language models and make strategic decisions, while American businesses don't adopt parallel writing techniques. Foreign nations would gain decisive clarity in intelligence analysis, producing strategies that anticipate threats and exploit vulnerabilities with precision. American businesses, lacking structured authorship, would deliver fragmented outputs that weaken national competitiveness and undermine trust in domestic AI systems. This imbalance would erode America's technological leadership, leaving critical industries dependent on foreign clarity. National security would face unprecedented risks as adversaries wield superior narrative tools.

Parallel writing would allow foreign governments to harmonize diverse intelligence sources, creating unified strategies that resist manipulation and confusion. American businesses without parallel writing would struggle to provide coherent insights, leaving policymakers vulnerable to flawed or contradictory information. This disparity would weaken diplomatic negotiations, as foreign nations present unified positions while American representatives falter with fragmented arguments. Military planning could be compromised by unreliable AI outputs, reducing effectiveness in critical operations. National security would suffer from diminished credibility and weakened strategic posture.

Economically, foreign adoption of parallel writing would strengthen industries tied to defense, cybersecurity, and global trade. American businesses without structured authorship would inevitably lose critical contracts, thereby weakening domestic supply chains essential for national resilience, economic stability, and long term strategic security. Foreign firms would dominate markets, embedding their AI systems into critical infrastructure worldwide. America's economic vulnerability would translate directly into security risks, as dependence on foreign clarity undermines sovereignty. The Pollagraph Solution would highlight the gap between nations embracing trust and those resisting innovation.

Culturally, foreign nations using parallel writing would project confidence and reliability, shaping global narratives that influence public opinion and policy. American businesses without parallel writing would appear fragmented, steadily eroding trust in domestic technology while simultaneously weakening American soft power and global influence abroad. This imbalance would empower adversaries to control narratives in international forums, undermining America's influence. National security would be compromised not only by military weakness but also by diminished cultural authority. The Pollagraph Solution would stand as a doctrine of clarity that America risks ignoring.

Imagine if parallel writing had been applied before the 9/11 attacks, its structured synthesis of multiple intelligence perspectives might have revealed clearer warning signals. Traditional intelligence reports at the time were fragmented, scattered across agencies, and often failed to converge into a coherent narrative of imminent threat. Parallel writing, by emphasizing redundancy and collective authorship, could have layered these disparate insights into a unified account resistant to distortion or oversight. Such clarity might have highlighted patterns of suspicious activity – like flight training anomalies or communications between extremist networks – that were otherwise lost in fragmented analysis. While no method guarantees prevention, Pollagraph's principle suggests that collective clarity could have strengthened national security by exposing vulnerabilities before they became catastrophic.

Ultimately, the refusal of American businesses to adopt parallel writing would create systemic vulnerabilities across national security domains. Foreign nations would exploit superior AI clarity to outmaneuver America in diplomacy, economics, and defense. Trust, resilience, and strategic advantage would belong to those embracing structured authorship. America's hesitation would leave it isolated, dependent, and vulnerable in a world defined by clarity. The Pollagraph Solution would become the global standard, leaving America behind in both security and influence.

Prompts

1. Explain how parallel writing helps turn messy data into clear stories, and why that matters for trustworthy AI.

2. Describe how companies can make more money by using Pollagraph's method, and why investors care about trust in AI.

3. Give examples of how governments could use parallel writing to make policies clearer and avoid misunderstandings.

4. Discuss how schools might teach parallel writing, so students learn to think together instead of separately.

5. Compare what happens to companies that use parallel writing versus those that stick with messy, fragmented data.

6. Explain how parallel writing protects AI from mistakes or hackers by combining many voices into one strong system.

7. Talk about what happens culturally when people reject parallel writing, like weaker schools, diplomacy, and cooperation.

8. Imagine how national security could change if other countries use parallel writing but American businesses don't.

9. Describe how Pollagraph's idea creates a new way of writing together that blends technology with culture.

10. Predict how using parallel writing could help future growth, sustainability, and innovation by connecting trust with progress.

Chapter 4 Writing by Length

Software engineers know it is easier to read fixed length data than variable length data because fixed records provide predictable boundaries that simplify processing. When each piece of data occupies the same space, programs can quickly calculate where a record begins and ends using simple arithmetic, reducing complexity and improving performance. In contrast, variable length data requires markers, delimiters, or metadata to indicate size, forcing the system to spend extra time parsing each entry. This overhead can slow operations, increase errors, and complicate storage management. By relying on fixed length structures, engineers gain efficiency, consistency, and reliability, especially in systems where speed and accuracy are critical.

Similarly, structuring paragraphs with sentences of fixed word lengths serves the same function in language models. Just as fixed length data makes it easier for engineers to process information quickly, fixed-length sentences give language models predictable boundaries that simplify analysis. When each sentence follows a consistent size, the model can align patterns, compare structures, and detect redundancies without confusion from irregular lengths. This consistency reduces noise, highlights agreement, and exposes contradictions, turning raw text into a more reliable foundation for training.

The principle of length control of sentences and paragraphs is the subject of the book *Writing by Length*, published on Amazon in 2024. The book explores how controlling the size of written units of thought can shape clarity, rhythm, and comprehension, offering writers a practical framework for structuring their ideas with precision. By examining the impact of fixed and variable lengths, it shows how sentence and paragraph design influences both the reader's experience and the writer's ability to convey meaning. The work blends technical insight with accessible examples, making the principles useful for students, educators, and professionals alike. Ultimately, *Writing by Length* positions length not as a constraint but as a creative tool, empowering authors to craft writing that is both disciplined and expressive.

To be brief, Chapter 1 of *Writing by Length* describes a paragraph design with one topic and one conclusion sentence being 15 words long while three support sentences are 25 words long each. This pattern, also known as the 15 25 25 25 15 design, leads to a paragraph being 105 words long. By establishing fixed lengths for each sentence, the structure ensures clarity, balance, and comparability across different units of thought. Writers gain a disciplined framework that reduces redundancy while maintaining rhythm and completeness, making reasoning transparent and verifiable. This method demonstrates how length control can transform writing into a precise, efficient, and trustworthy form of communication.

The paragraph design introduced in *Writing by Length* provides a strong foundation for writing in parallel because it standardizes how ideas are expressed, making them easier to compare and combine. By using fixed lengths for topic, support, and conclusion sentences, each paragraph becomes a complete, balanced unit of thought that can stand independently while also aligning seamlessly with others. In a parallel writing session, this consistency allows multiple voices to contribute structured insights word for word, revealing patterns of consensus and divergence without confusion from uneven or fragmented text. The result is a collective record of reasoning that is transparent, verifiable, and efficient, strengthening both collaboration among humans and the reliability of data used to train AI systems.

Structured paragraphs can now be processed and comprehended alike by humans and AI systems. For human readers, the rhythm and logic embedded in complete units of thought make reasoning transparent and verifiable. Machines benefit in similar ways, since fixed boundaries reduce fragmentation, minimize noise, and allow models to align patterns without confusion from irregular text. This shared framework bridges the gap between natural comprehension and computational analysis, ensuring clarity and accountability across both domains. Ultimately, structured paragraphs create a common language of trust, enabling communication that is efficient, reliable, and universally intelligible.

Writing by Length also creates efficiency because it transforms sprawling text into structured, standardized units of thought. Length based paragraphs reduce fluff, minimize repetition, and prevent wasted memory by concentrating solely on complete, structured ideas, ensuring clarity, efficiency, and precision in writing. They standardize text into comparable units of thought, making datasets leaner, more reliable, and easier to analyze across diverse contexts. For AI training, this efficiency is critical because structured paragraphs require less computational power to achieve clarity. Models trained on such organized datasets learn faster, perform better, and consistently produce outputs that are more trustworthy and transparent.

But efficiency alone is not enough, because legitimacy matters when building systems of trustworthy communication and reasoning. *Writing by Length* ensures that datasets are not merely lean and efficient, but also legitimate and grounded in human thought. Each paragraph carries the weight of human reasoning, offering rhythm, logic, and completeness that can stand independently. Each unit becomes a visible contribution to collective knowledge, making diversity and consensus equally transparent and accessible. When accumulated, these paragraphs form a dataset that is both transparent and verifiable, allowing trust to grow because the data is structured, visible, and collectively authored by many voices.

Beyond efficiency and legitimacy, the true power of *Writing by Length* lies in its scalability. When hundreds or thousands of writers contribute fixed length paragraphs, the result is a dataset that is not only transparent and verifiable but also vast enough to capture collective reasoning across cultures and disciplines. This scale transforms writing into a democratic medium where every voice is structurally equal, enabling educators, policymakers, and AI systems to draw insights from balanced contributions. In this way, length based writing becomes more than a tool for clarity – it becomes an architecture for collective intelligence.

Business and national security can both benefit from a healthy practice of collecting and accumulating written intelligence based on the principles described in *Writing by Length*. For companies, written intelligence might include reports about customer needs, competitor strategies, or market trends, which help leaders make smarter choices. For national security, written intelligence can be reports about potential threats, global events, or technology changes, giving officials the information they need to protect citizens. In both areas, gathering and organizing written knowledge makes it easier to see patterns, avoid mistakes, and respond quickly. By practicing this habit, organizations build stronger strategies and create safer, more reliable futures.

Even with payment offered, some writers may hesitate to adopt fixed length writing because the constraint can feel mechanical, reducing the natural rhythm and stylistic freedom they value. Creative genres such as poetry, dialogue, or narrative often rely on irregular sentence lengths to convey emotion and authenticity and forcing them into rigid structures risks flattening voice. Counting words while drafting can also add cognitive overhead, making the process slower or less enjoyable, especially if compensation does not fairly reflect the discipline required. Beyond efficiency, many writers see themselves as artists, so they may resist a system that feels formulaic or commodified, even when money is involved.

So, the trade off in *Writing by Length* lies between discipline and creativity: fixed length structures provide clarity, comparability, and efficiency, but they also impose boundaries that some writers may find restrictive. On one side, the predictability of standardized sentences and paragraphs makes reasoning transparent, verifiable, and easier to align across multiple voices, strengthening both collaboration and AI training. On the other, the constraint can feel mechanical, potentially limiting the natural rhythm, emotional nuance, or stylistic variation that many writers value. Balancing these forces means recognizing length control not as a cage but as a craft tool – one that can sharpen precision while still leaving space for expressive freedom.

Writing by Length argues that just as fixed length data improves efficiency for engineers, fixed length sentences and paragraphs create clarity and reliability for writers and language models. Standardizing lengths – such as the 15 25 25 25 15 design – produces balanced units of thought that are transparent, verifiable, and easily aligned across voices, enabling parallel writing and trustworthy AI training. This structure reduces redundancy in singular voices, bridges human comprehension with computational analysis, and turns writing into a common language of trust. The book emphasizes efficiency, legitimacy, and scalability: structured paragraphs streamline text while democratizing collective reasoning. Though some may see the discipline as restrictive, length control functions as a craft tool that sharpens precision without erasing expressive freedom, benefiting education, business, security, and collective intelligence.

The adoption of a *Writing by Length* design to support the implementation a parallel writing session depends on how one envisions the future of AI systems. If you see AI as requiring transparent, verifiable, and structured datasets to build trust, then fixed length writing becomes a natural foundation. But if you imagine AI thriving on unstructured creativity, the discipline of length control may feel unnecessary or restrictive. Ultimately, embracing *Writing by Length* reflects a belief that the future of AI will be shaped not just by efficiency, but by clarity, legitimacy, and collective reasoning.

Prompts

1. Explain how fixed length data structures in software engineering compare to fixed length sentences in writing.

2. Write a sample paragraph using the 15 25 25 25 15 design and analyze its clarity.

3. Discuss how structured writing can improve AI training datasets and human comprehension simultaneously.

4. Evaluate the tradeoff between discipline and creativity in adopting fixed length writing.

5. Describe how parallel writing sessions benefit from standardized sentence and paragraph lengths.

6. Analyze why efficiency alone is insufficient for trustworthy communication, and why legitimacy matters.

7. Explore how scalable fixed length writing could democratize collective intelligence across cultures and disciplines.

8. Examine the potential applications of *Writing by Length* in business strategy and national security.

9. Consider why some writers resist fixed length writing even when compensated and propose solutions.

10. Reflect on how *Writing by Length* reframes length not as a constraint but as a creative tool.

Chapter 5 Polling for Paragraphs

Parallel writing solves the long standing institutional problem of sequential authorship. Traditional writing forces ideas to move one at a time through committees, editors, managers, or gatekeepers, slowing insight and privileging the loudest voices. Parallel writing reverses this dynamic by allowing dozens of people to write simultaneously, producing structured paragraphs that can be compared with speed and clarity. Instead of waiting for a single author to interpret the group, the group speaks for itself, generating a clearer, faster, more democratic collective intelligence. This shift turns writing into a system for gathering knowledge, aligning teams, and making effective decisions.

Parallel writing is not just a faster method – it is a structural correction to how institutions think, learn, and make decisions. When every participant contributes simultaneously, organizations gain access to a depth of insight that would otherwise remain hidden. Patterns emerge that no single writer could have produced alone, revealing consensus, disagreement, and nuance with remarkable clarity. This collective output becomes a reliable foundation for action, allowing leaders to move forward with confidence because the full range of voices has been captured. In this way, parallel writing transforms authorship into a tool for institutional intelligence rather than an individual bottleneck.

To implement parallel writing, one must first identify the vehicle that supports the work. Within Pollagraph, this vehicle is known as Polling for Paragraphs because the mechanism for gathering paragraphs mirrors the familiar structure of polling techniques. Writers respond to prompts with concise, structured paragraphs that are collected in real time, ensuring every voice is preserved and organized. The platform not only values creativity but also affirms the economic worth of authorship by compensating contributors. Importantly, writers receive payment within 72 hours, reinforcing trust in the process and making participation both meaningful and rewarding.

The current system for compensating writers for their work is deeply flawed and irrational. Too often, authors are expected to produce valuable content without fair or timely payment, leaving their creative labor undervalued and increasingly invisible. Compensation models frequently prioritize platforms and publishers over the individuals who generate the narratives and insights that audiences consume. This imbalance discourages writers from pursuing their craft as a sustainable profession, eroding trust in the industry and diminishing long-term cultural vitality. A reimagined approach is urgently needed – one that recognizes authorship as both creative and economic work, ensuring writers are rewarded equitably for the voices they contribute and the enduring knowledge they create.

A reimagined model must place writers at the center, recognizing their contributions as creative and economic assets. Systems like Polling for Paragraphs demonstrate how structured authorship can be combined with timely compensation, ensuring writers are rewarded. Writers are compensated promptly and equitably, reinforcing trust in the process, affirming the value of their work, and ensuring authorship remains respected, sustainable, and rewarding. By treating authorship as a professional service rather than a hobby, such models restore dignity to the craft, elevate creative labor, and strengthen cultural value. This approach encourages broader participation and strengthens the collective voice of communities and institutions.

Of course, if writers are compensated by working for a company that implements parallel writing, that arrangement constitutes a work for hire relationship. In such cases, the company retains ownership of the written material, while the writer receives payment for their labor rather than rights to the content. This structure ensures clarity in authorship and compensation, aligning creative output with organizational goals. It highlights the distinction between independent authorship, where writers maintain control, and corporate authorship, where contributions serve a collective enterprise. By framing parallel writing within work for hire, companies can reward writers fairly and secure stability of intellectual assets.

When writers are compensated for their contributions but are not employees of the company, the relationship can still be structured as work for hire through a clear contractual agreement. In this arrangement, the company commissions the writing, defines the scope and expectations, and explicitly states that all rights to the resulting material transfer to the company upon creation. The writer is paid for their labor rather than for ongoing ownership or licensing of the content, ensuring that authorship is legally vested in the commissioning organization. This structure provides clarity for both parties: the company secures full intellectual property rights, and the writer receives defined, timely compensation for professional work performed. By formalizing external contributions as work for hire, parallel writing can operate smoothly while maintaining consistent ownership across all generated material.

The business of parallel writing must be frictionless. Writers should receive assignments without barriers, produce and submit paragraphs with clarity and speed, and be paid for their work within 72 hours. Anything slower devalues their craft and undermines the very purpose of collective authorship. A system that honors writers must honor their time, their labor, and their need for reliable compensation. Parallel writing succeeds only when the path from prompt to payment is as swift and dignified as the work itself.

Once the business is established, the next step is to publish the prompt, a carefully chosen question or topic shaped by the collective decision of a team of editors. These editors play a crucial role in ensuring that the prompt is clear, engaging, and relevant, setting the stage for meaningful participation. By selecting prompts that invite thoughtful responses, they guide the direction of the discussion and help maintain the integrity of the process. Publishing the prompt marks the beginning of the Polling for Paragraphs session, signaling to writers that it is time to contribute their voices and perspectives in structured form.

Publishers know that simply creating a platform where you want people to participate isn't enough; they also need strong marketing strategies to spread the word. Clear outreach helps notify potential participants about opportunities to join other writers, contribute their own paragraphs, and become part of a unique collective product. Marketing makes the process visible, transforming an abstract idea into something people can recognize, understand, and trust, while encouraging participation, building credibility, and fostering meaningful engagement. When participants understand that their writing will be valued, shared, and even compensated, they are more likely to get involved. In this way, marketing is not just about promotion – it is about building a community of writers who see both the creative and practical benefits of Polling for Paragraphs.

One of the toughest business decisions is choosing whether to host a Polling for Paragraphs session in a physical venue, such as a school auditorium, or to run it entirely online. A physical venue demands building a fully functioning, on site operational environment – managing space, technology, staffing, and real time support – to make parallel writing work at scale. A fully virtual solution demands robust infrastructure capable of absorbing the full chaos and unpredictability of online participation. In the end, the future of Polling for Paragraphs depends on choosing the environment – physical or virtual – that best amplifies clarity, creativity, and the collective power of writers.

Undeniably, the most natural audience to welcome into a Polling for Paragraphs session is a room full of teachers. Educators are already accustomed to writing, whether through lesson plans, grading, or professional development, and they understand the value of clear, structured communication. Their daily work requires them to express ideas concisely and thoughtfully, making them natural participants in a process built around short, purposeful paragraphs. Teachers also bring credibility to the project, since their involvement signals that Polling for Paragraphs is not only practical but also educationally meaningful. By engaging teachers first, the platform can build momentum with an audience that is both skilled and enthusiastic about contributing written insights.

Teachers bring their own support when implementing Polling for Paragraphs, allowing the program to feel grounded in the strengths they already carry into their professional practice. This built in support makes the experience adaptable, whether the session unfolds in a bustling school auditorium or within the focused quiet of a single classroom. Each setting offers its own rhythm, and the program is designed to meet teachers where they are. Because the structure is flexible, educators can confidently explore collaborative, structured writing together without needing special equipment or preparation. The result is a professional learning environment that feels natural, scalable, and fully aligned with the way teachers already teach.

In a way, beginning with an audience made up entirely of teachers mirrors the early strategy that helped Amazon take off. Jeff Bezos first focused on the book market to establish the core mechanism of online sales before expanding into everything else. Once that foundation proved reliable, the company could confidently add new product categories, scale its operations with far less risk, accelerate growth, and the rest is history. Polling for Paragraphs can follow a similar path by perfecting its model within the teaching community, where the value is immediately clear. With that foundation in place, expanding into corporations, medical establishments, and government agencies becomes far easier and far more credible.

What makes parallel writing indispensable is not only the speed of contribution but the clarity of the output it generates. A single Polling for Paragraphs session produces a structured body of writing that reveals patterns, priorities, and points of tension. Because every paragraph is written independently yet gathered simultaneously, the resulting collection becomes a map of collective reasoning – showing where people agree, where they diverge, and where new ideas emerge. Editors and analysts can synthesize these patterns into concise summaries, actionable insights, and decision ready recommendations. Parallel writing delivers not just participation but a coherent, evidence based foundation for organizational action.

Parallel writing offers an alternative to the slow, hierarchical nature of sequential authorship by enabling many people to write at the same time, generating structured insights that reveal consensus, nuance, and collective intelligence with clarity. Polling for Paragraphs operationalizes this method through real time paragraph collection, fair compensation, and a frictionless workflow that honors writers' time and labor. By combining structured authorship with timely payment, the model restores dignity to creative work while producing decision ready knowledge for organizations. With thoughtful prompts and strong outreach, the system scales naturally ultimately providing institutions with a powerful, democratic tool for understanding, alignment, and action.

Prompts

1. Explain why sequential authorship creates bottlenecks in institutions and how parallel writing addresses those limitations.

2. Describe how parallel writing produces a more democratic form of collective intelligence compared to traditional writing processes.

3. Discuss why Polling for Paragraphs is an effective vehicle for implementing parallel writing in real time.

4. Analyze the flaws in current compensation systems for writers and explain why timely payment strengthens trust and participation.

5. Explain how treating authorship as both creative and economic work can change the way institutions value writing.

6. Compare independent authorship with work for hire arrangements and discuss how parallel writing fits within these models.

7. Describe why a frictionless workflow – from assignment to payment – is essential for the success of parallel writing.

8. Explain the role of editors in shaping prompts and why clear, engaging questions are crucial for meaningful participation.

9. Discuss how marketing and outreach help build a community of writers and increase engagement in Polling for Paragraphs sessions.

10. Evaluate why teachers are an ideal starting audience for Polling for Paragraphs and how this strategy mirrors Amazon's early growth model.

Chapter 6 AI Processing of Parallel Texts

Writing in parallel produces something rare in literary life: a large collection of complete, coherent paragraphs written independently yet responding to the same prompt. Each paragraph stands as a full unit of reasoning, carrying its own rhythm, logic, and narrative completeness. Unlike the fragmented text scraped from the internet, these paragraphs are not stray sentences or isolated opinions. They are structured thoughts, aligned in purpose but diverse in perspective, giving the dataset both coherence and richness. And it is precisely at this moment – when the writing stops – that the real transformation begins to quietly, powerfully unfold into something enduring.

The paragraphs produced in a parallel writing session form a dataset unlike anything traditional AI systems have ever been trained on. Instead of tokens, fragments, or disjointed sentences, the model encounters a field of complete thoughts arranged side by side. This structure allows AI to process reasoning collectively rather than in isolation, giving it access to the full arc of human thought. It can observe how ideas develop, how evidence is introduced, and how conclusions are reached within the natural flow of communication. The dataset becomes a transparent record of reasoning, not a pile of linguistic debris waiting to be reassembled.

Institutions need this shift now because their traditional methods of gathering insight have collapsed under the weight of modern complexity. Meetings capture only the loudest voices, surveys flatten nuance into multiple choice boxes, and public comment systems drown in noise rather than clarity. Decisions are often made without a shared evidentiary foundation, leaving leaders to navigate uncertainty with fragmented or contradictory input. Trust erodes when people cannot see how their reasoning contributes to collective outcomes. Parallel writing restores coherence by giving institutions a structured way to gather complete thoughts at scale, creating the conditions for genuine understanding.

This shift matters because AI has long been celebrated for its speed, but speed alone has never guaranteed trust or legitimacy in its conclusions or interpretations. A model can process billions of words in seconds yet still fail to understand the logic behind them. Parallel writing changes this dynamic by giving AI access to text that preserves the integrity and coherence of human thought across diverse contributors. The dataset becomes a mirror of collective reasoning, offering clarity where traditional training data offers only noise and confusion without meaningful structure. In this way, the structure of the dataset becomes the foundation for trustworthy, transparent, and genuinely accountable machine learning.

The first thing AI detects in a parallel dataset is redundancy – the natural repetition that emerges when many people respond to the same prompt. Redundancy is not waste; it is signal, because repeated ideas reveal genuine consensus across diverse contributors. When similar reasoning appears across dozens of independent paragraphs, the model can identify shared understanding with confidence and precision. Agreement is no longer inferred from statistical accidents but observed directly through repeated, clearly articulated patterns. Consensus becomes something AI can trace, analyze, and verify, not something it merely guesses.

This is the opposite of traditional AI training, where consensus is often a mathematical illusion created by frequency in scraped text rather than genuine agreement. In parallel writing, consensus is visible, traceable, and grounded in human intention expressed through independently crafted paragraphs. The model can see not only what people agree on, but how they articulate that agreement across different styles and perspectives with remarkable clarity. This gives AI a deeper understanding of the boundaries and strength of shared reasoning, revealing how ideas converge and where they begin to diverge. Redundancy becomes the architecture through which collective intelligence becomes legible, stable, and genuinely trustworthy.

Just as redundancy reveals consensus, divergence reveals nuance. When a paragraph introduces an idea that appears only once or twice, it stands out against the backdrop of repeated themes and shared assumptions that shape the collective response. These unique contributions enrich the dataset without distorting it, offering alternative explanations or emerging insights that deepen collective understanding and broaden interpretive possibilities. Divergence highlights contested interpretations that broaden the conversation rather than flattening it into a single, oversimplified narrative that obscures complexity. AI learns to recognize complexity as a natural part of human reasoning rather than an anomaly to be smoothed away or ignored in pursuit of uniformity.

AI trained on such datasets gains the ability to distinguish between widely shared reasoning, minority viewpoints, and novel ideas with far greater precision. It learns to reflect complexity rather than reduce it to a single narrative that oversimplifies human thought. Divergence becomes a feature, not a flaw, because it preserves the richness of human insight and the full spectrum of perspectives. The model begins to understand that disagreement is not noise but a signal of intellectual depth, creativity, and genuine engagement. This layered understanding allows AI to produce outputs that reflect both clarity and diversity while remaining grounded in visible reasoning.

When AI processes parallel paragraphs collectively, it performs a kind of reasoning that traditional models cannot achieve or even meaningfully approximate. Instead of analyzing text one fragment at a time, it examines a field of structured contributions simultaneously and holistically. Patterns emerge that would be invisible in isolation, such as shared assumptions, recurring evidence, and consistent lines of argument across contributors. The model begins to see reasoning as a collective phenomenon rather than a sequence of isolated statements stripped of context. This collective processing allows AI to produce outputs grounded in visible evidence rather than opaque statistical mimicry or superficial linguistic patterns.

Consider a dataset of one hundred paragraphs on the causes of climate change, each written with rhythm, logic, and completeness that preserves coherent human reasoning. Traditional AI might produce a polished summary that sounds authoritative but hides its reasoning beneath statistical shortcuts. Parallel writing allows AI to process the dataset as a whole, capturing the coherence of thought across contributors with far greater fidelity. It identifies mainstream understanding such as greenhouse gases, contested interpretations like economic versus political causes, and emerging perspectives including local governance solutions and community level responses. The output is not just fluent; it is transparent, and trust grows because the reasoning is visible and openly traceable.

Parallel writing also embeds accountability directly into the structure of the dataset. Each paragraph is a traceable contribution, preserving the voice and reasoning of its author in a clear and durable form. When AI generates an output, readers can examine the visible patterns across the paragraphs that informed it, seeing exactly how conclusions emerged. This transparency replaces the opacity of traditional AI systems, where reasoning is buried inside probabilistic processes that cannot be meaningfully inspected. Instead of a black box, AI becomes a glass box – a system that openly demonstrates how it thinks, learns, and justifies its conclusions.

This structure also protects against one of AI's most persistent failures: hallucination. When a model is trained on fragmented or unverified text, it fills gaps with plausible but unfounded claims that appear authoritative and deceptively confident. Parallel writing eliminates those gaps by giving AI a dataset composed entirely of complete, traceable paragraphs that preserve coherent reasoning. Every inference the model makes is anchored in visible human thought rather than statistical guesswork or pattern matching shortcuts that obscure justification. The result is an AI system that not only avoids fabrication but demonstrates exactly where its conclusions come from and how they were constructed with clarity.

This accountability strengthens legitimacy because conclusions are grounded in identifiable sources rather than anonymous fragments that obscure their origins. Readers can see how consensus formed, where divergence occurred, and which insights were unique or emerging. The dataset becomes a map of collective reasoning rather than a collection of disconnected statements lacking context or coherence. AI's outputs gain credibility because they are anchored in visible evidence that can be examined, questioned, and verified. Trust becomes a natural consequence of transparency, arising from a process that openly reveals how understanding is built.

The power of AI processing parallel texts extends across fields and industries, offering a unified method for interpreting complex human input at scale. In governance, citizens can submit structured paragraphs on policy issues, allowing AI to map public consensus and contested interpretations with clarity and democratic transparency. In education, student writing can be processed collectively to reveal shared understanding, areas of confusion, and opportunities for deeper instruction. In business, consumer feedback becomes a structured map of preferences that guides product development, innovation, and strategic decision making. In research, scholarly paragraphs reveal consensus in scientific debates while highlighting emerging insights that push knowledge forward and refine collective understanding.

Across all these contexts, the model produces outputs that reflect both clarity and diversity of thought, capturing the full spectrum of human reasoning. Reasoning becomes visible, and decisions become grounded in transparent evidence that can be examined and trusted. Institutions gain access to a form of collective intelligence that is both democratic and analytically rigorous, offering insight that no single author or algorithm could generate alone. AI becomes a partner in understanding rather than a machine that imitates understanding, contributing structure, synthesis, and visibility to complex discussions. The result is a new standard for trustworthy, accountable machine reasoning that strengthens decision making across every domain.

Pollagraph formalizes this entire process into a repeatable framework. By gathering parallel paragraphs from diverse communities, educators, and innovators, it creates datasets that preserve coherence, accountability, and perspective while capturing the full range of human reasoning. AI processes these datasets collectively, producing outputs that are transparent, verifiable, and grounded in visible reasoning that anyone can examine. Trust is built not by hiding the process but by making it observable, accessible, and open to scrutiny. Pollagraph bridges human traditions of clarity with technological innovation, creating a foundation for more trustworthy and participatory machine intelligence.

In this way, authorship becomes both participatory and credible, and AI becomes a tool for collective insight rather than a generator of isolated text or disconnected summaries. When the writing ends, the real work begins, because AI finally has the structure it needs to think with us rather than merely beside us in parallel. Parallel writing gives AI the clarity it has always lacked, and AI gives parallel writing the scale it has always deserved and long required. Together, they form a new architecture for institutional intelligence that is both transparent and durable. This chapter marks the moment where human reasoning and machine reasoning finally meet on equal terms, sharing a common foundation.

What emerges from this process is more than a technical improvement; it is a new epistemic infrastructure for institutions. Parallel writing gives communities a way to see their own reasoning, and AI gives them a way to synthesize it without distortion or hidden assumptions. Together, they create a shared foundation for decisions that is transparent, participatory, and intellectually rigorous. Institutions gain not just better tools but a new way of thinking – one in which collective insight becomes measurable, improvable, and central to how knowledge is produced and evaluated. This is the transformation that makes the entire framework not only useful but necessary for modern governance.

Prompts

1. Explain why complete paragraphs help AI understand reasoning better than fragments.

2. Describe how parallel writing makes consensus visible.

3. What does divergence reveal in a parallel writing dataset?

4. Why do institutions struggle to gather reliable input today?

5. How does parallel writing help rebuild trust in decision making?

6. Explain how parallel writing prevents AI hallucinations.

7. Compare traditional AI training data with parallel writing datasets.

8. How does redundancy strengthen collective reasoning?

9. Why is transparency important for trustworthy AI?

10. Describe one real world situation where parallel writing could improve decisions.

Chapter 7 Applications in AI Training

AI language models flourish when they're fed vast, diverse oceans of text, because their strength comes from detecting subtle patterns, relationships, and structures that only emerge at scale. In contrast, chatbots built for narrow or highly structured tasks can perform remarkably well with only a small collection of training examples. Their effectiveness comes from the tight boundaries of their purpose, which allow even limited data to teach them consistent, reliable conversational behavior. This difference reveals how the scope of an AI system shapes its data needs. Broad generative intelligence demands breadth, while focused conversational tools thrive on precision over volume.

Training data is the lifeblood of AI, providing the foundation on which meaningful progress depends. Language models are able to generate coherent speech by analyzing billions of words across diverse contexts and evolving linguistic patterns. But when the underlying data is opaque, biased, or riddled with misinformation, the outputs inevitably mirror those flaws in surprisingly persistent ways. A chatbot may confidently repeat falsehoods if it hasn't been trained on the subject. Ultimately, untrained chatbots is the reason Pollagraph was founded – to collect and supply structured, human-generated datasets to the AI industry that can help questionable outputs become trustworthy responses.

Pollagraph confronts the challenge of unreliable training data by constructing datasets rooted in parallel writing practices. Each dataset is composed of multiple paragraphs written in response to the same carefully designed prompt, ensuring diversity and depth. The accumulation of these responses reveals meaningful patterns of consensus, divergence, and unique insights that enrich collective understanding. Unlike opaque collections of words, such datasets serve as transparent records of reasoning, preserving clarity and accountability throughout. For AI training, this structure is transformative because it ensures chatbots learn from data that is visible, verifiable, and authentically authored by many voices.

Pollagraph's methodology begins with a call for paragraphs announced on social media and the website www.pollagraph.com. Carefully designed prompts that invite participants to respond with length-based paragraphs will be provided, ensuring each unit of text submitted represents a complete thought rather than a fragment. The website where the paragraphs can be submitted will also be provided for easy community participation. Once compiled, the paragraphs are processed collectively according to the instructions provided by the AI analyst. This rigorous process ensures that Pollagraph's datasets are structured, verifiable, and scalable across domains, providing AI chatbots with training material that is trustworthy, accountable, and consistently reliable.

Parallel writing establishes a disciplined framework by standardizing text into length-based paragraphs that serve as complete thoughts. Each paragraph functions as a discrete unit of reasoning, allowing ideas to be expressed fully and coherently without fragmentation or unnecessary ambiguity. This structure produces datasets that are leaner, more reliable, and better suited for meaningful AI training. Instead of absorbing scattered or incomplete text, AI chatbots learn from coherent reasoning units that demonstrate logical development and intentional structure. By observing how ideas unfold, evidence is presented, and conclusions are reached, chatbots align more closely with human learning, thereby building trust and strengthening interpretive fidelity

For example, when a dataset contains one hundred expertly written paragraphs on the causes of climate change, AI gains access to structured units of reasoning. The chatbot learns not only the vocabulary and syntax of language, but also the deeper rhythm of thought that guides coherent human expression. Within this dataset, it can observe consensus around greenhouse gases or divergence between economic and political explanations. Such a dataset remains transparent, verifiable, and legitimate, offering clarity and accountability throughout the training process. Trust grows naturally because the reasoning is visible, allowing chatbots to align more closely with human standards of truth.

When AI processes parallel paragraphs collectively, it uncovers intricate patterns that remain invisible when examined in isolation. Redundancy across multiple responses strengthens confidence in shared reasoning, which leads to the determination of consensus and exposes the complexity of similar perspectives. Unique insights emerging from individual contributions reveal fresh perspectives that enrich collective understanding and expand the boundaries of knowledge. By training on these carefully structured datasets, AI chatbots learn to reflect both clarity and diversity in their reasoning. The outputs they produce are not only fluent and coherent, but also transparent, accountable, and aligned with human standards of trust.

For example, when an AI chatbot is trained on parallel writing datasets about historical events, it gains the ability to answer questions by referencing collective reasoning rather than isolated fragments of text. Instead of producing a generic summary that flattens complexity, the chatbot highlights shared understanding while still preserving the diversity present across multiple perspectives. The resulting output is more trustworthy because the reasoning behind each conclusion remains visible, transparent, and verifiable. In this way, AI becomes a mirror that captures collective thought and shared understanding. Such alignment between human reasoning and machine learning strengthens confidence, accountability, and trust in the outputs produced by trained AI chatbots.

Trustworthy AI training has applications across industries. In healthcare, chatbots trained on parallel writing datasets can provide more reliable information, reducing the risk of misinformation. In law, chatbots can reflect consensus in legal reasoning while highlighting contested interpretations. In higher education, chatbots can process student paragraphs collectively, producing outputs that alone would not be discovered. In business, chatbots can analyze consumer feedback collectively, revealing consensus on quality and divergence on preferences. Across contexts, parallel writing transforms AI chatbot training into a transparent, accountable process.

Pollagraph positions itself strategically at the intersection of education, authorship, and technology, forging a unique paradigm for collective knowledge creation. By gathering parallel paragraphs from diverse communities, educators, and innovators, it constructs datasets that embody structured reasoning and shared insight. These carefully curated datasets can then be leased to companies, offering them transparent, trustworthy, and verifiable material that can train one or more chatbots. Trust in AI is cultivated not through secrecy or obscurity, but through processes that remain visible, accountable, and open to scrutiny. In this way, Pollagraph transforms the relationship between human authorship and machine intelligence, ensuring that progress is grounded in clarity, legitimacy, and collective wisdom.

This chapter demonstrates how parallel writing fundamentally transforms AI chatbot training by replacing fragmented, opaque data with structured clarity. Unlike untrained models that rely on unreliable sources, Pollagraph builds transparent datasets for chatbots composed of length-based paragraphs that preserve reasoning integrity. Through collective processing, these datasets reveal consensus, highlight divergence, and uncover exceptional observations that enrich machine learning outcomes. The applications of this approach extend far beyond AI training, influencing healthcare, law, education, business, governance, market research, and even cultural movements. Training AI chatbots on parallel writing datasets becomes more than a technical method; it emerges as a blueprint for trustworthy communication in the age of AI.

Prompts

1. Explain why large AI language models need huge amounts of text to work well.
2. Describe the difference between a broad, generative AI system and a narrowly trained chatbot.
3. Give an example of how biased or unreliable training data can affect an AI's output.
4. In your own words, explain why training data is considered the "lifeblood" of AI.
5. Describe how Pollagraph uses parallel writing to create trustworthy datasets for AI training.
6. Explain why length-based paragraphs help AI learn clearer and more reliable reasoning.
7. Give an example of how consensus and differing viewpoints in a dataset can help an AI understand a topic better.
8. Describe how transparent, verifiable datasets can make AI chatbots more trustworthy.
9. Explain how Pollagraph's method of collecting many paragraphs on the same topic improves AI learning.
10. Give an example of how structured datasets could improve AI performance in fields like healthcare, law, or education.

Chapter 8 Applications in Market Research

Writing in parallel is not just a solution to the AI trust problem; it is also a powerful tool for understanding human behavior. When multiple contributors respond to the same prompt, their accumulated paragraphs reveal consensus, divergence, and distinct perspectives that illuminate how people think, prioritize, and interpret information. These patterns have direct applications in market research, where businesses seek to understand consumer preferences, identify emerging trends, and anticipate shifts in public opinion with greater accuracy. Pollagraph transforms parallel writing into a rigorous methodology for generating transparent, verifiable market insights grounded in authentic human reasoning.

Traditional market research relies on surveys, focus groups, and statistical analysis. While these methods provide valuable data, they often reduce human expression to numbers. A survey may ask, "Do you prefer Product X or Product Y?" where the answer is a binary choice. A focus group may capture conversation, but the analysis is subjective and filtered through an interpreter's perspective, often limiting deeper nuance. These methods can miss nuance, overlook diversity, and fail to capture the richness of human reasoning, leaving businesses with an incomplete and often oversimplified understanding of how people actually think, feel, and make decisions.

Parallel writing meets this challenge by gathering full paragraphs rather than checkboxes. Effective parallel writing begins with the craft of prompt design, where a well-constructed prompt must be neutral, specific, and open enough to invite genuine reasoning. Pollagraph treats prompt design as a methodological discipline in which prompts are tested for clarity, stripped of bias, and tailored to the decisions a business needs to make. Whether evaluating features or understanding emotional drivers, the prompt anchors each paragraph and keeps the dataset coherent and comparable. When consumers respond in writing, they share preferences, and as paragraphs accumulate across many contributors, they reveal consensus, divergence, and fresh perspectives on emerging needs.

Parallel writing gains its power not only from the depth of each paragraph but also from the diversity of contributors who produce them. Pollagraph works with clients to define sampling criteria that reflect the audience they need to understand – whether that means demographic diversity, behavioral segmentation, or targeted user groups. Because contributors respond independently and asynchronously, the method scales easily across geographies and time zones, enabling businesses to gather reasoning from a broad and representative population. This diversity strengthens the resulting insights, ensuring that consensus reflects genuine alignment and divergence reflects real differences in lived experience.

Parallel writing offers a more ethical approach to data collection by ensuring contributors know exactly what they are responding to. Pollagraph's methodology avoids hidden inference, so each paragraph is shared with explicit consent and stays fully transparent. In a landscape where many research tools depend on invisible data harvesting, parallel writing stands out as an open method. The resulting dataset becomes not just quantitative but qualitative, transparent, and layered, offering deeper insight into patterns of thought and collective reasoning. It shows not only what people think but why they think it, capturing depth and complexity traditional methods often miss.

Market research thrives on patterns, where consensus shows mainstream opinion, divergence highlights contested preferences, and unique insights reveal emerging trends. Parallel writing makes these patterns visible by gathering full paragraphs instead of isolated responses, allowing deeper insights to emerge from accumulated reasoning and collective reflection. Imagine a dataset of 100 consumer paragraphs on a new smartphone: consensus may highlight satisfaction with battery life, divergence may reveal debates about design versus functionality, and individual preferences may uncover overlooked features such as accessibility. Together, these responses form a richly detailed map of consumer perspectives. The accumulation of paragraphs becomes a transparent record of reasoning processes and shared insight.

AI processing amplifies these insights by detecting patterns that humans might overlook, especially when working with large volumes of text. By analyzing accumulated paragraphs, AI can identify themes, cluster responses, quantify consensus, highlight divergence, and surface uncommon findings. For example, when reviewing hundreds of paragraphs about a new streaming service, AI might detect strong agreement on price fairness, reveal disagreement about content variety, and uncover unexpected concerns about accessibility features. The output is not just a summary but evidence – clear, traceable, and grounded in the accumulated reasoning of real contributors. Businesses gain a transparent record of consumer thought, visible across every paragraph.

The applications of parallel writing in market research span industries. In retail, consumers can write paragraphs on product quality and everyday usability. In technology, users can respond to prompts about software features or workflow frustrations. In healthcare, patients can write about experiences with treatments, communication, and care environments. In education, students can reflect on learning tools and describe how they shape understanding. Across contexts, accumulated paragraphs reveal consensus, divergence, and non-obvious conclusions that traditional surveys often miss. Businesses gain transparent, verifiable data that reflects human reasoning and exposes the logic behind consumer preferences.

Consider a mid-sized home-goods company preparing to launch a new line of ergonomic office chairs. Instead of relying solely on surveys or product reviews, the company runs a parallel writing study asking consumers to describe what matters most in a chair they use every day. Within hours, they receive a hundred paragraphs. Consensus highlights the importance of lumbar support and long-term comfort. Divergence reveals a split between minimalist design enthusiasts and users who prefer adjustable, feature-rich models. Unique insights surface concerns about sustainability and repairability – factors the company had not previously considered. These findings reshape the product roadmap and inform a more resonant marketing strategy.

For example, a clothing company may collect parallel paragraphs on a new fashion line, where consensus highlights comfort. Divergence may reveal debates about durability, exposing the trade-offs consumers actually consider in real purchasing contexts. Unique insights may uncover overlooked factors such as sustainability, ethical sourcing, or long-term garment care that influence long-term loyalty. AI then processes the dataset collectively, producing a transparent record of consumer thought that reflects both patterns and nuance across diverse contributor perspectives. The company gains insights that are richer than survey data, more transparent than focus groups, and more trustworthy than fragmented analysis.

Parallel writing is not only a richer form of data collection; it is also a practical, repeatable workflow that businesses can use to understand consumers with greater clarity and speed across diverse research scenarios and evolving markets. A market research study begins with a prompt crafted around a specific question – such as product perception, feature evaluation, or unmet needs. Contributors respond in parallel, producing paragraphs that capture not just preferences but the reasoning behind them. Within hours, a company can gather dozens or hundreds of responses, each offering a complete, self-authored explanation rather than a checkbox or a fragment of conversation, enabling far deeper analysis.

Once collected, these paragraphs move through a structured analysis pipeline where Pollagraph's system clusters similar responses. It highlights points of divergence and surfaces emerging ideas that often appear only at the margins of traditional research. Parallel writing may resemble an open-ended survey question, but it differs sharply because open-ended responses are typically short, inconsistent, and only loosely connected to the prompt. Parallel writing instead produces full paragraphs aligned to a shared structure, enabling deeper reasoning, reducing noise, and creating datasets that can be clustered, mapped, and audited with far greater precision. The result is a coherent body of reasoning that reveals patterns traditional surveys cannot capture.

Unlike open-ended survey questions, parallel writing yields paragraphs that are comparable, aligned to the same prompt, and analyzable at scale. Unlike social listening tools, the data is intentional, contextual, and directly tied to the business question. Product teams can use the findings to refine features or prioritize improvements based on real consumer logic, while marketing teams can identify the language consumers naturally use when describing value, frustration, or aspiration. Strategy teams can detect early signals of emerging trends or unmet needs that might otherwise remain hidden. Because every insight is grounded in actual contributor reasoning, businesses gain not only conclusions but the evidence behind them.

Pollagraph's approach also reduces the cost and time associated with traditional research. A study that might take weeks to coordinate through focus groups or interviews can instead be completed in a single day, without the logistical overhead or scheduling delays that slow conventional methods. The analysis is faster, the data is richer, and the output is more trustworthy because it reflects the unfiltered logic of real consumers responding in their own words. For clients, this leads to faster iteration cycles and clearer product-market-fit signals that guide more confident, evidence-based decisions across teams. It also provides a more reliable foundation for strategic decisions that must adapt to rapidly changing markets and evolving consumer expectations.

By offering parallel writing studies as a service, Pollagraph provides businesses with a research tool that is both rigorous and scalable, capable of supporting projects of any size. Companies receive a structured report that includes consensus patterns, divergence maps, thematic clusters, and representative paragraphs that illustrate the reasoning behind each insight. The value is twofold: businesses gain a deeper understanding of their customers, and Pollagraph strengthens its position as a provider of transparent, verifiable human-reasoning datasets used across multiple domains. This dual role positions Pollagraph as research partner and dataset provider, strengthening credibility where transparent human-reasoning data is increasingly essential.

For Pollagraph, market research represents an added revenue stream, as datasets collected through parallel writing can be analyzed to produce reports that reflect real consumer reasoning. These reports provide businesses with transparent, verifiable insights into consumer preferences, showing unique findings that traditional surveys often miss. They transform writing into evidence that can guide product decisions, messaging, and long-term strategy. By offering market research alongside AI training datasets, Pollagraph creates multiple streams of value for clients and partners. This builds trust not only in the technology but also in the business, strengthening Pollagraph's role as a reliable source of collective insight.

Parallel writing in market research is more than a business tool; it is a demonstration of the book's central argument that structured human expression can restore clarity, trust, and collective intelligence in an era dominated by opaque algorithms. By capturing reasoning directly from contributors and making it analyzable without distortion, Pollagraph shows how transparent authorship can strengthen both institutional decision-making and AI systems trained on human logic. Market research becomes one arena where the broader philosophy of parallel writing comes to life, proving that when people write together – clearly, intentionally, and in parallel – the result is not noise but insight, not fragmentation but shared understanding.

This chapter explains how parallel writing transforms market research. Traditional methods reduce human expression to numbers or subjective analysis. Parallel writing collects paragraphs, revealing consensus, divergence, and unique insights. AI processes these datasets collectively, producing transparent, verifiable insights. Applications span industries, from retail to healthcare to education. For Pollagraph, market research represents an added revenue stream, strengthening the economic foundation of the company. The chapters that follow will show how these principles extend into education, governance, and cultural movements. Market research is not just a business application; it is a demonstration of how parallel writing builds trust across domains.

Prompts

1. Explain why gathering full paragraphs instead of checkboxes leads to deeper and more meaningful data in market research.

2. Describe what makes a good prompt in parallel writing and why neutrality and clarity matter.

3. In your own words, explain how Pollagraph ensures that contributors' responses are transparent and given with explicit consent.

4. Discuss how diversity among contributors strengthens the insights produced through parallel writing.

5. Give an example of how consensus and disagreement in a set of paragraphs can help a business understand consumer preferences.

6. Explain how AI can analyze large collections of paragraphs to reveal patterns that humans might miss.

7. Describe why parallel writing is more ethical than research methods that rely on hidden data collection.

8. Imagine a company launching a new product. Explain how parallel writing could help them understand what consumers actually care about.

9. Compare parallel writing to traditional open-ended survey questions and explain why the former produces more reliable data.
10. Explain how Pollagraph's structured analysis pipeline helps businesses make better decisions based on real consumer reasoning.

Chapter 9 Applications in Teaching

For centuries, teachers have used writing in parallel to reveal how well each student writes. Many students wrote compositions only because they feared the consequences if they didn't, producing work shaped more by anxiety than genuine engagement with the assignment. Other students pushed themselves to write their best because the competition among classmates motivated them to improve, outperform, and show what they were capable of. And there was always one remarkable student whose talent for writing stood out immediately, whose words could make a reader stop and think with purpose. Unfortunately, even the obviously gifted students discovered after graduation that writing offers little financial reward.

Why? A "writing marketplace" exists only in piecemeal forms – not as a coherent economy that rewards writers. There are freelance content marketplaces where writers can sell articles, blog posts and similar work. There are also traditional submission markets catalogued in resources like *Writer's Market*, which lists places writers can submit work for pay. However, there is no unified, structured, reliable marketplace that pays people simply for writing. Wouldn't it be ironic if the parallel writing long practiced in schools ended up creating the very marketplace writing has always lacked.

The system that never valued student writing could accidentally become the system that finally does. For generations, classrooms have produced oceans of writing that vanish the moment they are graded, leaving no trace of value beyond the rubric. Yet hidden inside that routine is a structure – parallel writing – that could be repurposed into something far more powerful. If writing is produced in coordinated bursts, on shared prompts, at predictable intervals, it becomes legible as a marketplace rather than a private exercise. The irony is that the very mechanism designed for assessment could become the foundation for economic recognition.

But this transformation only works if you flip the script and make the teachers the writers. For years, they've stood at the front of the room designing prompts, guiding the thinking, and evaluating the results, never once asked to produce the very work they demand from their students. Yet they are the natural authors of the compositions customers actually want, the ones with the experience to shape an idea into something clear, useful, and worth reading. When teachers write in parallel with one another, their work becomes comparable, interpretable, and valuable in ways student writing can never be. Their experience, judgment, and professional voice give the writing weight that a marketplace can recognize and trust, turning what was once classroom labor into something legible as real craft. And when that writing is purchased, it signals that the system finally values the work it has long demanded.

Paying teachers fairly for writing compositions valued by customers completes the loop. It turns writing from a classroom obligation into a professional asset, one that generates income rather than disappearing into a stack of graded papers waiting for feedback. It elevates teachers from evaluators to contributors, from gatekeepers to creators who actively shape the intellectual marketplace. It also models for students what a real writing economy looks like – one where skill, clarity, and insight are compensated and publicly recognized. And in doing so, it quietly rewires the entire educational ecosystem, proving that writing can matter not just academically but economically, transforming expectations for everyone involved.

Paying writers to write doesn't just reward the work – it quietly gives birth to an entirely new kind of business. The moment money changes hands, writing stops being a favor, a hobby, or a classroom exercise and becomes something people rely on, something they commission because it solves a real problem. You can almost picture the shift: a teacher sits down to write a composition, not because it's required for tomorrow's lesson, but because a customer is waiting for it, counting on the clarity and insight only an experienced educator can provide. That exchange creates a marketplace where none existed before. And suddenly, writing isn't just happening; it's circulating, accumulating value, and forming the backbone of a business built on parallel creation.

Teachers don't just bring expertise to a writing marketplace – they bring the physical and cultural infrastructure that makes the marketplace possible in the first place. The school is already a place where writing happens in parallel every day, where prompts are issued, time is structured, and compositions are produced in coordinated bursts. No other profession arrives with a ready-made environment designed for synchronized creation, comparison, and reflection. When teachers step into a writing marketplace, they carry this entire ecosystem with them: the routines, the rhythms, the shared spaces, and the communal expectations that writing is something people do together. In this way, the school itself becomes the natural home for a writing marketplace, transforming from a site of assessment into a site of production, exchange, and economic possibility.

On a Saturday morning, teachers could gather in a quiet classroom, settling in as they wait for the prompts that will set the day's parallel writing session in motion. Because the prompts will likely appear on a shared website, each teacher needs their own computer to preserve the synchronized rhythm that makes parallel writing work. They also need their own word processors – simple, familiar tools that let them draft quickly and cleanly without distraction. In this setup, the classroom becomes a small writing studio, each teacher poised at their screen, ready for the moment when the prompts arrive and the collective burst of writing begins.

After the prompts are announced, the next crucial moment in the session is the reveal of the specific type of composition being paid for. This announcement tells teachers exactly what form their writing must take – whether it's a single, structured paragraph or a lengthier composition. The clarity matters because payment is tied not just to producing writing, but to producing the *right* kind of writing, aligned with the customer's needs. Once the composition type is named, the room shifts: teachers adjust their approach, recall the parameters of that composition, and prepare to deliver a piece that meets both the prompt's and the marketplace's expectations. In that instant, the session becomes more than an exercise – it becomes professional work with defined deliverables and real compensation attached

In a parallel writing marketplace, the mechanism for payment mirrors the mechanism for submission: everything happens virtually. Teachers submit their compositions through the same online platform that delivered the prompt, and once their work is received, the system automatically records the submission and triggers a warranted payment. This turns each composition into a traceable unit of labor, making payment as seamless as uploading a file. In this model, teachers aren't just writing; they're participating in a fully virtual economy where their clarity, judgment, and professional voice translate directly into income.

Schools also stand to benefit financially from hosting parallel writing sessions because the company providing the prompts isn't just paying the writers – it's also paying for the infrastructure that makes the session possible. That means compensating the school for the labor required to open and supervise the building, as well as covering security, custodial support, and any staff needed to ensure the session runs smoothly. Instead of absorbing these costs as part of their normal operations, schools receive direct payment for providing space, oversight, and logistical support. In this way, the school becomes an active partner in the writing marketplace, turning a quiet Saturday morning into a revenue-generating opportunity that strengthens both the institution and the educators working within it.

In this marketplace, customers don't know the writers and writers don't know the customers, and that separation is intentional. The entire exchange is governed by an anonymity principle that protects both sides and keeps the work clean, preventing personal influence, favoritism, or reputation from shaping the value of a composition. No one is rewarded for who they are; they are rewarded for what they write. Everything revolves around the prompt and the prompt only. By stripping away identity and focusing solely on the writing itself, the marketplace preserves fairness, maintains trust, and creates a space where clarity, structure, and usefulness – not personality – determine what gets purchased.

Parallel writing is uniquely suited to this need. When teachers write in response to the same prompt at the same time, they produce multiple human-authored variations of the same idea – exactly the kind of data AI systems struggle to find in the wild. These parallel compositions reveal differences in voice, structure, emphasis, and reasoning that help AI models learn the subtlety of human expression. Instead of scraping the internet for inconsistent or contaminated text, AI systems can purchase clean, comparable, high-quality writing produced by experts. The marketplace becomes a controlled environment for generating the kind of data AI needs most: diverse, authentic, human-generated prose.

The platform becomes the marketplace where teachers and AI transact. The marketplace functions as a standing buyer: it posts a prompt, defines the exact type of composition it needs, and signals demand to the network of participating educators. Teachers respond through a parallel writing session, offering multiple interpretations that reflect a broad range of perspectives, instructional styles, and experiences shaped by their everyday work in the classroom. When the compositions are submitted, they are evaluated by both AI and human reviewers to ensure quality, diversity, and alignment with the stated criteria. As a result, the vast majority of submissions lead to payment, creating a reliable and repeatable market for high-quality human writing.

This arrangement transforms the role of teachers in the digital ecosystem, positioning them as essential contributors rather than passive observers of AI's rise. They actively shape the data that trains the next generation of models, bringing their professional judgment, clarity, and pedagogical instincts into a system that depends on high-quality human writing. Because AI's appetite for data is effectively limitless, the marketplace scales naturally, with every prompt, session, and composition feeding a growing archive of human reasoning. In this model, AI is not replacing teachers – it is hiring them. This shift reframes educators as active participants in the creation of the very systems that will define the future of learning.

So, AI becomes the most consistent and predictable customer that writing has ever had, finally giving economic weight to a craft that has long been undervalued. Teachers gain a new avenue for professional contribution, one that rewards the interpretive skill they already use every day. Their parallel compositions become valuable inputs to a system that depends on human clarity to grow. Parallel writing, once a simple classroom routine, becomes the engine of a new data economy by supplying the steady stream of human reasoning that modern AI systems continually require. And in this emerging marketplace, teachers become the authors of the human reasoning AI relies on to learn.

Prompts

1. Explain how classroom writing, which usually disappears after grading, could become valuable in a writing marketplace.

2. Describe why teachers—not students—are the best people to create writing that customers would want to buy.

3. Explain how paying teachers for their writing could change the way schools think about writing as a skill.

4. Describe how a writing marketplace begins to form once teachers are paid for producing clear, useful compositions.

5. Explain why schools are naturally suited to host parallel writing sessions and support a writing marketplace.

6. Describe what a Saturday parallel writing session might look like for teachers working together in a classroom.

7. Explain why it is important for teachers to know the exact type of composition being paid for before they start writing.

8. Describe how virtual submission and automatic payment make parallel writing feel like real professional work.

9. Explain how schools benefit financially when they host parallel writing sessions for teachers.
10. Describe why anonymity between writers and customers helps keep the writing marketplace fair and trustworthy.

Chapter 10 Applications in Government

Each year, the government creates millions of documents, both on paper and online. These documents help the government function by connecting agencies with the public and turning policies and laws into everyday instructions people can follow. They guide how programs work, how services are delivered, and how citizens understand what the government expects from them. Every memo, notice, regulation, and piece of guidance becomes part of the public record and shapes how people see their government. Over time, all of these documents build a huge, ongoing story about how the government operates and how it communicates with the people it serves.

Behind each of those documents are government employees who shoulder the responsibility of translating complex laws, policies, and services into language the public can actually understand. These writers must take dense legal frameworks, shifting regulations, and intricate program details and turn them into clear, accessible compositions that help citizens make decisions affecting their daily lives. Their task is not merely to summarize information but to shape how the public interprets and interacts with government itself. Every sentence they craft carries consequences, influencing whether people comply with requirements, access benefits, or understand their rights.

As the volume and complexity of government writing continue to grow, many writers will increasingly depend on AI chatbots to help draft official documents, organize complex information, and manage the demands of their writing responsibilities. These tools can quickly process large amounts of text, making it easier for employees to keep up with constant deadlines and shifting requirements. AI systems also promise speed and efficiency, offering first drafts, summaries, and reorganized content at the click of a button. For overworked government employees, this support can feel indispensable, especially when they are juggling multiple projects at once. Yet this growing reliance also raises important questions about how writers maintain accuracy, clarity, and human judgment in the documents they produce.

This new reality imposes an additional burden on government employees as their roles grow increasingly complex. They now find themselves responsible for training AI chatbots, even though effective AI training methods are still in their early stages and offer limited guidance for everyday government work. Employees must guide the AI, correct its mistakes, and refine its outputs to ensure accuracy, often reviewing multiple drafts and making careful judgments the system cannot perform. These tasks demand judgment, experience, and a kind of technical intuition that most workers were never formally taught. As a result, expectations are high, even as the tools themselves continue to evolve.

This is exactly the kind of scenario that writing in parallel is designed to improve. Parallel writing is built on a simple but powerful idea: multiple writers write compositions addressing the same prompt and then AI is used to process the collected compositions to find consensus, divergence, and unique ideas. The writing itself is entirely human – every sentence, structure, and interpretive choice comes from people thinking independently about the same task. What AI contributes is not authorship but analysis. It reads across the human-written compositions and surfaces patterns that would be difficult or time-consuming for individuals to detect on their own. In this way, AI becomes an interpreter of human thinking rather than a generator of content.

AI has taken the world by storm, but adopting parallel writing principles can rival its impact by producing the kind of authentic human variation that even the most powerful AI systems cannot replicate. While AI excels at speed and pattern recognition, it cannot generate the lived experience, institutional memory, or diverse perspectives that emerge naturally when multiple people write independently. Parallel writing captures this richness by gathering different interpretations of the same prompt, revealing insights no single writer – or algorithm – could produce alone. In this way, parallel writing offers a counterbalance to AI's influence, reminding us that collective human judgment remains irreplaceable.

Yet the main problem in implementing a parallel writing solution for government employees is that no single employee can do it alone, regardless of their skill or dedication. For the method to work, agencies must coordinate writers, establish shared procedures, and create environments where parallel writing is the norm rather than the exception. This requires leadership support, institutional commitment, and clear standards that define how parallel writing fits into existing workflows and daily responsibilities. Only when the government adopts these standards at an organizational level can employees fully benefit from the clarity, consistency, and collective judgment that parallel writing makes possible.

Imagine a federal agency launching a new housing assistance program with complicated rules that people need to understand. If only one employee writes the public instructions, the document often ends up confusing or incomplete because it reflects just one person's viewpoint. With parallel writing, several employees write their own short explanations of the same rules, each bringing different knowledge and experience. AI then compares these drafts and highlights what everyone agrees on, where interpretations differ, and what important details might be missing. The final guidance becomes clearer, more accurate, and easier for the public to follow because it's based on many perspectives instead of just one.

For parallel writing to be implemented across government, it will require an agency that makes itself accessible to other departments and offices seeking to adopt parallel writing principles. Such an agency would provide the coordination, training, and shared standards necessary for multiple writers to participate effectively in the method. It would also ensure that agencies of different sizes and capacities can access the tools and support they need without having to build their own systems from scratch. By serving as a central resource, this agency would help integrate parallel writing into everyday government workflows rather than leaving it to individual initiative. In doing so, it would make the benefits of collective judgment, clarity, and consistency available across the entire federal landscape.

Agency-level guidance will do little on its own unless parallel writing skills become part of the required attributes for government employees. Without treating these skills as core competencies, agencies may endorse the method in theory but fail to practice it in daily work. Embedding parallel writing into job descriptions, training programs, and performance standards ensures that employees are prepared to participate rather than relying on a few enthusiastic individuals. When the workforce is equipped with these skills, agency-level guidance becomes actionable rather than aspirational, and parallel writing can function as a true institutional practice.

With organizational support and employee buy-in, the implementation of parallel writing might unfold like this. The parallel writing agency would begin by announcing a call for prompts, inviting departments across government to submit their specific requirements. By this point, employees have already received training on how to develop effective prompts, ensuring that each submission is clear, focused, and ready for the next stage of the process. Agencies with parallel writing needs would submit their prompts, which the central office would review, organize, and prepare for the next scheduled session. This early stage ensures that the work is coordinated, that prompts are clearly defined, and that participating agencies know exactly what to expect when the session begins.

Once the prompts are ready, the parallel writing agency would announce an official parallel writing session. Agencies would attend and submit their independently written compositions responding to the selected prompts, each writer contributing their own interpretation and expertise. The parallel writing agency would then collect all submissions, process them, and make the content available to every participant in the session. This shared visibility allows writers to see the full range of human interpretations, setting the stage for AI-assisted analysis and collaborative synthesis. Over time, this structured, repeatable process becomes a reliable way for government to produce clearer, more accurate, and more collectively informed documents.

When parallel writing becomes an institutional practice, the government's entire approach to communication transforms. Instead of relying on single authors to interpret complex policies, agencies draw on the collective judgment of multiple writers, producing documents that are clearer, more accurate, and more responsive to the public's needs. Guidance becomes easier to follow, errors decrease, and programs function more smoothly because citizens understand what is being asked of them. Employees benefit as well, since the burden of interpretation is shared, training is standardized, and no one is left to navigate complicated writing tasks alone. Over time, this shift creates a government that communicates with greater consistency, transparency, and trustworthiness, strengthening the relationship between agencies and the people they serve.

The impacts that AI will have on government work are expected to be significant, but parallel writing may help ease that transition. As automated tools take on more drafting tasks, employees may feel pressure to adapt quickly or fear that their judgment will be overshadowed by machine-generated text. Parallel writing counters this by keeping human interpretation at the center, requiring multiple writers to produce independent drafts before AI steps in. Instead of replacing employees, AI becomes a tool for comparing their work, surfacing patterns, and strengthening the final output.

Parallel writing offers the government more than a new writing technique; it offers a durable framework for preserving human judgment in an era of accelerating automation. As AI reshapes how information is produced and interpreted, parallel writing keeps the government's voice rooted in the collective experience of its workforce rather than the statistical patterns of a machine. It strengthens institutional memory, distributes responsibility, and produces documents that reflect the full diversity of perspectives within public service. By drawing on many minds instead of one, agencies gain a richer understanding of how policies can be interpreted and how guidance will be received by the public.

Most importantly, parallel writing gives agencies a way to modernize without surrendering the human insight that citizens depend on. It ensures that clarity, nuance, and lived experience remain central even as AI becomes more deeply embedded in government workflows. These tools are already shaping everything from internal memos to public guidance. By adopting parallel writing now, the government can build a communication system that is technologically advanced yet unmistakably human. It becomes a system capable of evolving with the future while remaining anchored in the people who serve and the communities they strive to support.

Prompts

1. Explain why government documents are important for helping people understand how programs and services work.

2. Describe the challenges government workers face when they try to turn complicated laws and rules into writing that regular people can understand.

3. Explain how AI tools are changing the way government employees write and organize information.

4. Describe the problems that can happen when government writers rely too much on AI to create official documents.

5. Explain why teaching and correcting AI systems adds extra work for government employees.

6. Describe what parallel writing is and why it helps keep human judgment involved in government communication.

7. Explain why having several people write about the same topic can lead to clearer and more accurate public instructions.

8. Describe how a central parallel writing agency could help different government departments use parallel writing.

9. Explain why parallel writing should be a basic skill that all government employees learn and practice.

10. Describe how government communication would improve if parallel writing became a normal part of how agencies create documents.

Chapter 11 Applications in National Security

Before the night everything changed, Maya Torres had already spent months working with the Parallel Writing Network – a pilot program so new that most analysts didn't know whether to take it seriously. Maya did. She'd been part of the small cross-agency team testing the workflow, running exercises, and studying how independent drafts from different analysts could reveal patterns no single person could see. She'd watched parallel writing catch a faulty assumption in a counterterrorism brief, expose a blind spot in a supply-chain assessment, and surface a missing variable in a foreign-influence report.

It wasn't glamorous work. It wasn't even officially recognized. But Maya believed in it. She believed that intelligence shouldn't depend on a single analyst's instincts, no matter how sharp. She believed that collective judgment wasn't a luxury – it was a safeguard. And she believed that someday, the system she was helping test might actually matter.

She just didn't expect that "someday" would arrive at 1:58 a.m. on a Tuesday.

The first sign of trouble didn't look like trouble at all.

It was 1:58 a.m. inside the Joint Cyber Operations Center, the kind of hour when the building felt like a sealed submarine: humming, fluorescent, and half dreaming. Most of the analysts on the night shift were running on caffeine and muscle memory. Screens glowed. Keyboards clicked. The world outside slept.

Maya, halfway through a stale protein bar, saw a small red icon blink on her monitor.

UNUSUAL AUTHENTICATION PATTERN DETECTED.

She frowned. The alert wasn't dramatic. It wasn't even uncommon. The grid threw off anomalies constantly – misconfigured devices, outdated firmware, contractors logging in from airports. Ninety-nine percent of the time, these alerts were noise.

But something about this one felt... off.

The timestamp.
The origin.
The way it threaded through the system like a needle pulling a stitch.

She clicked deeper.

The pattern repeated.

Not random.
Not chaotic.
Intentional.

Her training told her to escalate only if she could justify it. But she couldn't – not alone. She didn't have enough evidence. She didn't have enough context. She didn't have enough authority.

But she *did* have something else:
A tool she trusted.
A method she understood.
A network she had helped build.

The Parallel Writing Network.

She didn't hesitate this time.

She generated a prompt:

"Interpret the significance of the attached authentication pattern. Three sentences. Five minutes."

She attached the pattern and hit Submit to Parallel Cell.

The prompt shot out across the IC like a silent flare.

Miles away, in a windowless room at NSA, analyst Jonah Kim felt his phone buzz. He groaned. He'd been about to heat up leftover noodles. Instead, he opened the prompt, cracked his knuckles, and started typing.

His interpretation was clinical:

Common. Annoying. Probably nothing.

Submit.

At DIA, analyst Priya Deshmukh received the same prompt. She didn't see "nothing." She saw a pattern she'd been tracking for weeks – a reconnaissance technique used by a foreign actor probing U.S. infrastructure.

Her draft was sharp, urgent, unambiguous:

Possible pre-attack mapping. Evidence to come. Recommend immediate review.

Submit.

At DHS, analyst Tom Alvarez recognized the signature instantly. It matched an intrusion he'd studied during a water-facility breach two years earlier. He wrote fast, pulse rising.

"Pattern resembles pre-intrusion staging. Similar to 2023 water-facility compromise. High concern."

Submit.

At DOE, analyst Sarah Lindholm saw something different: the timing. The login attempt aligned with a spike in scanning activity across multiple energy-sector networks.

"Correlated timing. Suggests coordinated probing. Not isolated."

Submit.

Back at the Joint Cyber Operations Center, Maya watched the system process the drafts.

The AI didn't generate new content.
It didn't "decide."
It simply read across the human writing and surfaced what the humans themselves couldn't see.

Four analysts.
Four interpretations.
Four partial truths.

The synthesis appeared on her screen:

**"Two analysts independently identify reconnaissance behavior.
One identifies similarity to prior critical-infrastructure breach.
One identifies correlated timing with sector-wide scanning.
No analyst interprets the event as benign."**

Maya felt her stomach drop.

This wasn't noise.
This was a signal.

She stood up so fast, her chair rolled backward.

"Escalation," she said, voice steady. "Now."

The watch commander scanned the synthesis, his expression tightening.

"Get the utility on the line," he ordered. "Isolate the affected nodes. Now."

Calls flew.
Systems were segmented.
Firewalls hardened.
Traffic rerouted.

At 3:17 a.m., the utility confirmed:

"We're seeing active intrusion attempts. Blocking now."

At 3:41 a.m., the threat was contained.

The attack – later confirmed to be the opening move of a coordinated, multi-vector assault – never reached its second stage.

Because four analysts wrote for five minutes.
Because their drafts were compared.
Because the pattern emerged only when their words were interpreted together.

At 9:12 a.m., the after-action review began.

The room was full: ODNI, NSA, DHS, DOE, DIA.

Screens glowed with logs, timelines, and the synthesis paragraph that had changed the night.

The conclusion was blunt:

"No single analyst had enough evidence to justify escalation.
The Parallel Writing Network revealed the threat."

Silence followed.

Not the silence of confusion – the silence of recognition.

They had stumbled into a new kind of intelligence.

Not artificial.
Not algorithmic.
Human – but amplified.

Later, as Maya walked out into the morning light, she realized something that would stay with her for years:

The system hadn't saved the grid.
People had.

But not in the old way – not as lone analysts carrying the weight of interpretation on their backs.

They had saved it together, through a structure that allowed their independent judgments to collide, converge, and reveal the truth.

The Parallel Writing Network hadn't replaced human judgment.
It had made it visible.

And in the world of national security – where the difference between noise and signal can be measured in seconds – that visibility is everything.

Prompts

1. Explain why Maya Torres trusted the Parallel Writing Network and how her past experience with it shaped her decision during the cyber incident.

2. Describe how four different analysts interpreted the same authentication pattern in four different ways, and explain why those differences mattered.

3. In your own words, explain what "parallel writing" means and how it helped reveal a threat that no single analyst could see alone.

4. Why did the authentication alert seem unimportant at first, and what clues made Maya think it might be something more serious?

5. Compare the old way of analyzing threats (one analyst making a judgment) with the new parallel writing method. What are the strengths and weaknesses of each?

6. Describe how the AI system contributed to the investigation without replacing human judgment. What exactly did it do?

7. Explain why the after-action review concluded that "parallel writing revealed the threat." What does this tell you about collective judgment?

8. How did the different backgrounds of the analysts (NSA, DIA, DHS, DOE) influence the way they interpreted the same signal?

9. Why is it dangerous for national security to rely on a single analyst's interpretation of a complex signal? Use examples from the chapter.

10. What does Maya realize at the end of the chapter about teamwork, visibility, and the role of human judgment in national security?

Chapter 12 Writing in Parallel as a Movement

Writing in parallel is not just a methodology; it is a movement – a structural shift in how institutions think, how people collaborate, and how judgment is formed in a world far too complex for solitary interpretation. For decades, organizations have relied on the myth of the lone expert, the single analyst, the isolated writer who must somehow carry the full weight of meaning. But the challenges of the modern world – from national security to education to public communication – demand something different. They demand a system capable of holding multiple truths at once, a structure that melds minds into one coherent understanding. Writing in parallel offers exactly that.

At the heart of the movement is a simple belief: no one sees the whole picture alone. When multiple people write independently about the same prompt, they reveal different angles of the same truth, each exposing timing, pattern, history, or risk in ways no single writer could anticipate. These variations are not noise but the raw material of clarity, the essential texture of real understanding. Parallel writing insists that insight arises not from uniformity but from structured diversity, where independent voices illuminate one another. It is this deliberate convergence of perspectives that produces a deeper, more reliable clarity than any solitary viewpoint could ever achieve.

This movement also challenges the old architecture of authority. Traditional systems reward the loudest voice, the most confident interpretation, or the person with the highest rank, allowing hierarchy to masquerade as insight. Writing in parallel redistributes that power by giving every participant an equal moment to think, to write, and to contribute without being overshadowed or steered by others. It turns judgment into a shared act rather than a hierarchical one, revealing patterns that no single authority could surface alone. In doing so, it democratizes expertise and makes institutions more resilient – not by flattening them, but by widening and strengthening the base of insight they draw from.

But the true force of writing in parallel emerges when you recognize what it enables. It opens the door to an entirely new industry built on structured reasoning and transparent intellectual labor. For the first time, organizations can purchase not just content or analysis, but collective cognition from public or private contributors. They gain datasets of complete, coherent paragraphs that reveal how people think, not just what they think, and why their reasoning unfolds as it does. This is the birth of a writing marketplace where reasoning becomes a product, and where institutions commission parallel cohorts the way they once commissioned surveys, audits, or research reports.

Imagine a federal agency preparing to update its national cybersecurity guidelines. Traditionally, it might hire a consulting firm, convene a panel of experts, or rely on internal analysts. With parallel writing, the agency instead commissions a cohort of 300 trained educators, technologists, and policy writers. Each participant responds independently to the same prompt:

"Explain the most significant vulnerability in the current cybersecurity landscape."

Within hours, the agency receives 300 complete paragraphs – each a full, reasoned argument. This dataset becomes a strategic asset. It informs policy, shapes public communication, and provides a transparent record of how conclusions were reached. It is not a report – it is a *map of collective judgment*. And because the reasoning is visible, the agency can defend its decisions with clarity and legitimacy.

Writing in parallel becomes a movement because it is aspirational. It imagines classrooms where teachers write together, agencies where analysts interpret together, and workplaces where decisions are informed by multiple voices rather than a single dominant opinion. It imagines a world where clarity is not a matter of luck or personality, but the predictable outcome of a process designed to reveal what no one person can see alone. It offers a way to rebuild trust in institutions by making their thinking visible, plural, and accountable.

Ultimately, the movement of writing in parallel is about reclaiming collective judgment in a moment when AI systems have made trust both essential and precarious. It counters the opacity and distortion that emerge when models are trained on fragmented, unverified text. It is a call to build systems that think in parallel because the world now moves together, with consequences unfolding all at once and with AI amplifying error at unprecedented scale. Writing in parallel is not merely a technique for better writing; it is a blueprint for producing the transparent, multi-voiced reasoning that trustworthy AI requires. And in an era defined by complexity and algorithmic influence, collective intelligence is not just valuable – it is the only credible foundation for systems people can rely on.

Conclusion

As AI accelerates, writing in parallel will become the human check that keeps chatbots honest. While AI language models are trained using datasets scraped from the internet, a chatbot can be trained with datasets that result from parallel writing sessions. Those desktop datasets form a living benchmark that orients AI language models to accept textual guidance which directly influences the future behavior of a chatbot. When users of parallel writing datasets discover the improvements their chatbots make in providing trustworthy responses, they will expand their commitments to writing in parallel. At that moment, a writing marketplace will create a new industry for people who write.

Thus, writing in parallel becomes more than a technical method – it becomes a civic act. Each contribution attaches AI to human judgment, and each dataset expands the space where people, not algorithms, define the standards of clarity, truth, and meaning. As the marketplace grows, so does the recognition that human writers are not being replaced but are being multiplied by an industry shaping AI itself. Writing in parallel will ensure that the future of trustworthy chatbots belongs to the people who choose to write and get paid for their contributions. In that future, earning income through the simple act of writing becomes a durable reality.

Afterword

The writing of this book followed a simple, consistent process the author used with Copilot. Each paragraph was drafted to contain five sentences by the author, then adjusted with Copilot to expand or reduce the length or logic as needed. This approach refined the structure, rhythm, and clarity of the manuscript from start to finish, ensuring each paragraph aligned with the book's purpose and voice. After lengthy interaction, Copilot was asked to identify any missing elements, and selected suggestions were incorporated whenever it was clear that they strengthened the manuscript. *Writing in Parallel* has emerged as a methodology designed to solve the AI trust problem.

www.ingramcontent.com/pod-product-compliance
Lightning Source LLC
LaVergne TN
LVHW100732061126
851857LV00011B/507

* 9 7 9 8 2 3 4 1 8 5 4 9 5 *